MW01200761

Politics Strangely Warmed

Politics Strangely Warmed

Political Theology in the Wesleyan Spirit

GREGORY R. COATES

Foreword by Charles E. Gutenson

WIPF & STOCK · Eugene, Oregon

POLITICS STRANGELY WARMED
Political Theology in the Wesleyan Spirit

Wipf and Stock
An Imprint of Wipf and Stock Publishers
199 W. 8th Ave., Suite 3
Eugene, OR 97401

www.wipfandstock.com

ISBN 13: 978-1-62564-522-7

Manufactured in the U.S.A.   01/20/2015

To Dad

Contents

Foreword

GIVEN THE PREPONDERANCE OF political theologies that exist today, it has been a constant source of annoyance to me that there is
so much promise in the work of John Wesley and the subsequent
Wesleyan tradition, and yet so little written on how that promise
might be mined. While one cannot expect that shortfall to be made
up in a single volume, I am delighted to see a former student, Greg
Coates, take up the question of what might inform a Wesleyan political theology. Coates has done us an important service in elevating the question of how the followers of Wesley might articulate
the relationship between Christian faith and political structures in
a way that avoids the simplistic descent into "right" or "left" readings. First and foremost, Coates reminds us that Wesley's thought
is far too complex to be so easily co-opted.

As my own work in theology has evolved, particularly in the
somewhat broader field of public theology, I have become increasingly persuaded that one of the great shortfalls of the church in the
twenty-first century is the lack of a sound understanding of the
relationship of Christian faith to the public structures that order
our life together. We followers of Jesus have allowed ourselves to
become as politically divided as the culture at large. And all too
often, we read the events of our day-to-day world guided much
more by our political ideology than by our Christian faith. In fact,
as Robert Bellah noted nearly fifty years ago now, in far too many
cases we have entangled our Christian faith and our political commitments to the point that we can hardly tell them apart anymore.

Wesley, and Coates as he examines him, makes it crystal clear that any and all efforts to organize and structure society is subject to the Lordship of Christ and the values that are implied by that. One can only imagine the harsh words Wesley would have for us today in light of our tendencies to become self-centered and individualistic in our accumulation of luxuries as we deny our obligations to care for the poor. For Wesley, this was not a mere hypothetical belief, but a commitment to a way of life that demonstrated values consistent with those beliefs.

Perhaps one of the central components of Wesley's theology that is ripe for bringing into the service of political theology is his doctrine of Christian perfection, or as it is often known, the doctrine of entire sanctification. If one takes the Lordship of Christ over all aspects of human life and couples it with Wesley's soteriology, one finds a potent basis from which to call for social transformation. First, one must recognize with Wesley that the claim "Jesus is Lord" is a cosmological claim about the state of the entire world, not just a claim about personal piety. Second, one might summarize the doctrine of sanctification by saying that Wesley firmly believed that God aims to empower followers of Christ by the power of the Holy Spirit in order to live together in the ways God intends for us. I think Coates rightly helps us to see this when he speaks of the importance of Wesley's narrative of salvation for understanding political relations, structures, and goals. His discussion is invaluable regarding the way in which social justice and personal salvation were inseparable in the early holiness movement.

Be sure to pay attention not just to Coates' treatment of the underlying theology of Wesley, but also note the way in which Coates assesses the impact of Wesley on the thinking of B. T. Roberts and the conclusions Roberts draws in favor of what must be characterized as a populist stance. In short, Coates shows how taking seriously the "in God's image-ness" of all people created in Roberts an intense desire to see the political agency of all realized. And when he says all, his point is particularly to be sure we do not overlook those on the margins for whatever reason. Political systems too easily become slanted in favor of the powerful, but this can never be acceptable to one who fully realizes that all humans are bearers of the divine image.

It is a great delight to be asked to write the foreword to a book like this—one dealing with a subject so important for the contemporary church. How can we Christians balance the triad of temptations to either: 1) grow frustrated with politics and withdraw, as if the Lordship of Christ did not extend here, 2) to simplify the debates by merely adopting one position or the other ideology, or 3) to so thoroughly entangle our faith and our politics that we can no longer tell them apart? Well, a good beginning is to look at someone like Wesley, a man whose position evolved with time and who readily adopted positions that might be characterized as sometimes "left" and sometimes "right." A good beginning on that task is taking the time to carefully appropriate the insights laid out for us by Coates in this valuable book. I'd go so far as to say the conclusion alone is worth the price of admission!

—Charles E. Gutenson

Preface

WHEN I TELL MY fellow students at Garrett-Evangelical Theological Seminary in Evanston, Illinois, that I am currently attending my third seminary within the Methodist tradition, it typically raises eyebrows. Even more so once they find that my Master of Divinity came from the evangelically-oriented Asbury Theological Seminary in the rolling hills of Kentucky's bluegrass. There, where Highway 68 winds past the little "heaven on earth" that is Wilmore, Kentucky, the holiness tradition of my childhood continues to thrive, producing women and men devoted to "spreading Scriptural holiness across the land." My Master of Theology degree, however, is stamped with the seal of the Barthian and postliberal Duke Divinity School of Durham, North Carolina. Here the Divinity School sits contiguous with the iconic Duke Chapel, which, beginning in 1930, had been built deliberately separated from the African-American part of downtown Durham. And now, as a student at the mainline Methodist seminary Garrett-Evangelical on the North Shore of Chicagoland, I still walk through the architecture of white privilege, bespeaking a tradition of Methodists who established their own enclave catering to many of Chicago's most prestigious and respectable families.[1] Within each is embedded a unique history, theology, and yes, political persuasion.

Such remarkable diversity among those who all claim to be the theological heirs of John Wesley is truly breathtaking. My decision to write this book, which predominantly represents my

---

1. Finke and Stark, *Churching of America*, 172.

master's thesis written from 2012 to 2013 at Duke Divinity School under the guidance of Dr. Randy Maddox, has been motivated by the question, "Is there such a thing as a Wesleyan political theology?" Currently, the landscape of Wesleyanism seems about as divided as it can be. Of course, I do not pretend to be able to bridge such an enormous gap, but I am deeply concerned that the partisan alliances so ubiquitous in our national conversation—if one can even call it a conversation any longer—should not be allowed to trump the language and narrative of the Christian faith, which calls us to live on earth with "one Lord, one faith, one baptism" (Eph 4:56).

I am not the first to ask this question. In fact, Wesleyan scholars have for decades been looking back to the life of our progenitor in the faith, John Welsey, and to other Wesleyan figures for guidance on how the church ought to witness in the political sphere. Rather than seeking to reinvent the wheel, I have drawn from these scholars, particularly from two of the most persuasive—Theodore Weber and Howard Snyder—in an effort to chart a map forward. It is a tentative map, one likely to be criticized and reworked by minds far more brilliant than my own, yet in a day when many disciples of Christ know how to speak American better than they know how to speak Christian, I believe this conversation to be vital to the life and mission of the church.

Introduction

Recovering a Wesleyan Political Theology

THE WORDS "POLITICAL THEOLOGY" may seem like an odd pairing to many. The discipline of political science is certainly well established, having acquired its own vocabulary, rules, scholars, and practitioners. Likewise, theology stands upon its own time-honored tradition, having once been acknowledged in medieval Europe as the "queen of the sciences." But what are we to make of this hybrid "political theology"? To those unfamiliar with the term and those who are committed to the idea of the separation of church and state, the very notion may sound appalling.

In brief, political theology attempts to articulate the proper relationship between religious belief and the structure of society. Thus, the discipline involves asking crucial ethical questions such as "To what extent is it proper for Christians to engage in the political process of the nation-state? What, if anything, does the gospel message have to say regarding modern issues such as terrorism, militarism, global warming, immigration, and the like? Are certain forms of government polity more compatible with biblical teaching than others?" However, beyond even these questions, political theology is concerned foremost with the flourishing of human life and how this common life we share with one another in society ought to be best arranged in order to promote such flourishing. Theologians since the Apostle Paul and Augustine of Hippo and up to the present day have engaged in questions of political theology, for ultimately all questions of the common life are concerned with how to best live out the central ethic of Christianity to "love thy neighbor." Stated succinctly, the theologians William Cavanaugh and Peter Scott define political theology as "the analysis and criticism of political arrangements (including cultural-psychological, social and economic aspects) from the perspective of differing interpretations of God's ways with the world."[1]

Of course, some today would prefer that religion and politics maintain as much distance as possible from one another. According to the (increasingly rare) champions of secularization theory, the rise of rational thought and scientific analysis will eventually dissipate the fog of blind religious faith, freeing humanity to establish a political system founded exclusively on humanistic, rational principles of toleration. For those who do insist on preserving some sort of belief system, matters of faith must be kept "private"—in the home, the church, and the family, but most certainly not allowed to spill out onto Capitol Hill or Wall Street or even Main Street.

Yet, despite such predictions of increasing secularization, the role of religion in the public arena has only increased in recent years, as has the academic interest in the role of religion in public life. When the Twin Towers crumbled into dust on that Tuesday morning in 2001, suddenly the world took note that religion is not by any means a private phenomenon. In response, suddenly many secularists scrambled to understand the nature of religious faith and how it motivates public action. They learned what theologians and believers had known all along: that faith has never been and never can be a merely "private" matter. As Elizabeth Phillips has stated, "[P]olitical theology is entirely unavoidable. People's thought, discourse and practices related to political arrangements will inevitably be shaped by their thought, discourse and practices related to the divine, and vice versa."[2] This is an inevitability. Theologians and people of faith have also long known this: bad theology leads to the destruction of our shared life; good theology promotes the flourishing of our shared common life. Thus,

---

1. Scott and Cavanaugh, *Blackwell Companion to Political Theology*, 2.

2. Phillips, *Political Theology*, 3.

political theology matters tremendously. The widespread recognition of this fact within academic circles largely explains why the discipline has experienced something of a renaissance since 9/11.

Nevertheless, for all that is being written in the discipline of Christian political theology in our own day, relatively little of it comes explicitly from the Wesleyan tradition. Choose any given introduction to political theology, and you will likely find plenty of references to Augustine, Aquinas, Luther, Calvin, and more recent scholars such as Reinhold Niebuhr, William Cavanaugh, Stanley Hauerwas, and John Howard Yoder. Yet with the possible exception of Hauerwas, whose theology is decidedly more Anabaptist than Wesleyan, none of these represent the tradition of John Wesley and the Methodists.

Perhaps this lamentable state of affairs can be attributed to the fact that John Wesley himself—always the practical theologian—never systematically articulated an explicit political theology in the same way that other theologians have done. Theodore Weber insightfully observes the same:

> Lutherans can speak the language of Two Kingdoms if they choose to do so, Roman Catholics that of natural law, Calvinists that of covenant and federalism, and Mennonites that of a community of faithful disciples living under the law of Christ, but Wesleyans have no common symbols of discourse deriving from their own theological tradition with which to think and speak as *Wesleyans* about the meaning of political reality and responsibility.[3]

In this book, I propose one example of a figure in Methodist history who represents the best of the Wesleyan tradition as it is lived out in the public sphere: Benjamin Titus Roberts, the founder of the Free Methodist Church. My contention is that Roberts represents a clear example of Wesleyan civic engagement and political theology. Drawing from the thesis of Theodore Weber as proposed in his masterful book *Politics in the Order of Salvation*, I hope to show that Roberts' work as the populist organizer of the Farmers' Alliance in New York represents a concrete manifestation of the

3. Weber, *Politics in the Order of Salvation*, 17.

implications of Wesley's doctrine of the political image of God. Indeed, Roberts' activism, when properly understood, was more faithful to Wesleyan theology than John Wesley himself, although this can undoubtedly be at least partly attributed to geographical and historical circumstances.

This brief book is divided into three chapters. In the first, I survey the various interpretations of John Wesley's politics and suggest some key distinctions that must be kept in mind whenever interpreting his thinking about theological politics. This will also serve as an introduction into the issues surrounding the study of Wesleyan political theology. In chapter 2, drawing especially from the exhaustive research of Howard Snyder in his groundbreaking work *Populist Saints*, I turn to B. T. Roberts and offer an account of his involvement in the Farmers' Alliance in New York and the larger populist movement in the mid- to late nineteenth century. Roberts' populist activism, as well as the theological reflection that undergirded it, presents us with a historically concrete form of uniquely Wesleyan political praxis. And finally, in chapter 3, returning once more to the thesis of Theodore Weber, I will argue why B. T. Roberts ought to be recognized as a prime example in Methodist history of one who lived out the implications of Wesley's doctrine of the political image of God.

The bulk of this short volume is historical theology, but my hope is that by learning from history and theology, we may be inspired to act more faithfully in the present. Like a good Wesleyan, I am always concerned with the practical. Theory is all well and good, but how does it change the way we live? Therefore, if you picked up this book hoping to read something less theoretical and more relevant to our situation in twenty-first-century American society, all is not lost. Skip to the end, as they say, and read the conclusion. There, I set aside the academic tone and the long footnotes and instead offer what I hope will be some useful, concrete suggestions for how to navigate today's partisan political landscape like Wesleyans and, more importantly, like earnest Christians.

1

Will the Real John Wesley Please Stand Up?

A Survey of the Various Interpretations of Wesley's Political Theology[1]

THE LIFE AND WORK of John Wesley, father of the eighteenth-century Methodist movement in England, left an indelible mark on the history of Christianity, especially in Europe and North America. The impact of the Methodist movement reshaped not only the spiritual, but also the political landscape of England and the United States. Indeed, some have even argued that were it not for the impact of Wesley and the Methodists, England would have been plunged into a bloody revolution similar to that experienced in eighteenth-century France.[2] Yet, despite its historical significance, the political theology of John Wesley is notoriously difficult to pinpoint. While some scholars have argued Wesley was

1. A version of this chapter first appeared as a peer-reviewed article under the title "Will the Real John Wesley Please Stand Up? A Survey of the Varying Interpretations of John Wesley's Political Theology." *Aldersgate Papers* 10 (2012) 12–29. Reprinted by permission.

2. This theory was first proposed by the French historian Élie Halévy in 1906. For an English translation, see Halévy, *Birth of Methodism in England*.

1

a deeply conservative High Church Tory thoroughly committed to king and country, others have depicted him as a proto-Marxist liberation theologian.[3] While most scholars espouse an interpretation between these two extremes, this is a debate that will likely continue for decades to come.

What are we to make of these radically different interpretations of John Wesley's political theology? In this chapter, I will first provide a survey of the differing interpretations of Wesley's political theology offered by scholars in recent years, paying particularly close attention to the work of Leon Hynson, Theodore Jennings, and Theodore Weber. Second, I will suggest three crucial distinctions that must be kept clear for any proper interpretation of Wesley's political theology.

INTERPRETATIONS OF WESLEY'S POLITICS

Throughout most of the nineteenth and early twentieth centuries, scholars depicted John Wesley as a High Church Tory typified by the following four characteristics: 1) commitment to the doctrine of divine right, 2) the conviction that God (rather than the people) chooses kings, 3) the practice of passive obedience to authority, and 4) a profound fear of democratic liberalism as the seedbed for anarchy.[4] Ample evidence in Wesley's letters, sermons, and writings can be cited in support of this view, including, most obviously, Wesley's famous statement in 1775, "I am a High Churchman, the son of a High Churchman, bred up from my childhood in the highest notions of passive obedience and non-resistance."[5] As Jason Vickers notes about Wesleyan scholarship in the first half of the twentieth century, "In what was among the most influential early

---

3. For a conservative interpretation of Wesley's political theology, see Weber, *Politics in the Order of Salvation*, and for a liberationist reading of Wesley, see Jennings, *Good News to the Poor*. Both of these will be examined in greater detail later in this chapter.

4. Vickers, *Wesley: A Guide for the Perplexed*, 61–62.

5. John Wesley, "Letter to William Legge," June 14, 1775, in Wesley, *Letters of the Rev. John Wesley*, 6:156; hereafter referred to as *Letters*.

twentieth-century monographs of Wesley's political philosophy, Maldwyn Edwards' *John Wesley and the Eighteenth Century* begins with the simple and straightforward declaration, 'John Wesley was a Tory.'"[6] Due to the preponderance of evidence in Wesley's writings for this theory, this facile depiction of Wesley as a Tory, articulated by scholars such as Frederick Norwood, Richard Cameron, and William Warren Sweet, remained largely unchallenged until the early 1970s.

In the last forty years, however, scholars have argued for a more nuanced view of Wesley's politics, in some cases citing him as a proto-liberal democrat committed to natural rights. Leon Hynson was among the first to reinterpret Wesley's political convictions in this vein. Hynson argues that Wesley underwent a radical transformation in his political position throughout his life, particularly during a transitionary period between the years 1734 and 1764.[7] In his younger years, Wesley reflected the conservative Tory views of his father, but the late Wesley had greater appreciation for individual human liberty as a God-given right and grew in sympathy with democratic movements.[8] As a foundation for his argument, Hynson points to Wesley's increasing willingness to critique his government on issues such as slavery and the plight of the nation's poor, and also to advocate for natural rights and human liberty.

Hynson's argument challenged the accepted view by stressing five specific and interrelated points: 1) Wesley wrote as a champion of human liberty; 2) he supported the human regulation of kingly authority inasmuch as he favored a limited constitutional monarchy such as that which had been established in England over and against an absolute monarchy, 3) he opposed the pre-Glorious Revolution notion of the divine right of kings, 4) he supported the monarchy only insofar as it protected and defended basic human

---

6. Vickers, *Wesley: A Guide for the Perplexed*, 62.

7. Hynson, "Human Liberty as a Divine Right," 57–85.

8. See Hynson, "John Wesley's Concept," 36–46; ibid., "John Wesley and Political Reality," 37–42.

rights, and 5) Wesley's view of the liberty of conscience undercut his early appeals to passive obedience.[9]

Central to Hynson's argument is the conviction that Wesley underwent a significant period of change during the middle years of his life, a thesis later to be built upon by Theodore Weber. In summary, over and against the view that Wesley was purely Tory, Hynson concludes, "Wesley's central commitment was not to his country, his king, or negatively, his distaste for republican governments, but his dedication to the full liberties of his land, liberties both in church and state, both personal and social."[10] Here Hynson opens the door for future interpretations of Wesley as a proto-liberal democrat committed to human rights, a thesis quite palatable to American Methodist scholars seeking to recruit the founder of their church as a supporter of classically liberal and democratic values.

In his book *Good News to the Poor: John Wesley's Evangelical Economics* (published in 1990), Theodore W. Jennings interprets John Wesley as a forerunner to modern liberation theology. Agreeing that Wesley placed strong emphasis on human liberty and natural rights,[11] Jennings builds on Hynson's thesis and radically expands it to depict Wesley as a proto-Marxist. Jennings draws attention to the many sermons and letters Wesley wrote condemning the ownership of private property and instead extolling the early church of Acts 2–4, including their practice of holding all possessions in common, as exemplary for modern Methodists.

Jennings argues that God's preferential option for the poor takes center stage in Wesley's theology and becomes the litmus test for earnest Christian belief: "Thus the question of solidarity with the poor was ultimately a question of the authenticity of the Christian's confession of faith."[12] As for Wesley's defense of the

9. Hynson, "John Wesley and Political Reality," 38.

10. Ibid., 41.

11. Jennings writes, "For Wesley the question of human rights is the decisive norm for the development of a political ethic" (Jennings, *Good News for the Poor*, 200).

12. Ibid., 130.

monarchy, Jennings explains that Wesley compromised with the political establishment in order to protect the young and vulnerable Methodist movement from being associated with other anarchist movements. But Jennings contends that Wesley's monarchism never took a central place in his sermons.[13]

It is essential to note that Jennings differs from Hynson in his point of departure. Whereas Hynson is primarily concerned with Wesley's political convictions, Jennings is more interested in what he calls Wesley's "evangelical economics." One might say that Hynson reads Wesley's economics in light of his politics, but Jennings reads Wesley's politics in light of his economics. And this is a deliberate interpretive choice on the part of Jennings, who argues, "One of the conditions for a rereading of Wesley in this connection is the move from an emphasis on *political* issues to an emphasis on *economic* issues as significant for the general themes of social ethics."[14] Jennings explicitly states that this orientation situates his own scholarship within the tradition of liberation theology.

From this starting point, then, Jennings argues that Wesley took a critical stance toward the given economic structures of his day and used both his pen and his pulpit to "demystify" wealth and power. Wesley became intensely critical of the economics of private property as popularized by the thought of John Locke[15] and instead turned to the early church as an alternative economic model favoring common property. This theological persuasion led Wesley to actively engage in political and structural advocacy in the hope of developing "a positive ethic that will alter the given

---

13. Ibid., 206–209.

14. Ibid., 19. Emphasis added.

15. Thomas Madron notes the points of difference between Wesley and Locke: "Unlike John Locke, whose ideas dominated much of the eighteenth-century political and economic thought, Wesley refused to elaborate a theory for the absolute protection of property rights . . . For Locke, property became an inalienable right which must be defended. For Wesley, on the other hand, property was never an inalienable right; any person holds property only as a steward of God" (Madron, "John Wesley on Economics," 107). For a primary source, see John Wesley, "Sermon 50: The Use of Money," in Wesley, *The Bicentennial Edition of the Works of John Wesley*, 2:263–80; *The Bicentennial Edition of the Works of John Wesley* hereafter referred to as *Works*.

socioeconomic reality" of his day "that breaks the spell of 'private property' and leads to a redistribution of wealth whose criterion is the welfare of the poor."[16]

Jennings and Hynson both view Wesley as limited by the context of his own day. They readily recognize the ways in which Wesley's politics do not align with modern liberal values, but they highlight elements of his thought that resonate with later developments. As Hynson concludes, "From the vantage point of our historical position, some of Wesley's assumptions and beliefs are seen to be faulty, but his commitment to human liberty is a luminous and penetrating valuation of man."[17] Jennings would agree, yet push further to argue that a modern reading of Wesley will properly situate him as the progenitor of liberation theology.[18]

---

16. Jennings, *Good News to the Poor*, 25.

17. Hynson, "John Wesley and Political Reality," 42,

18. As Jennings is well aware, a proper emphasis upon Wesley's interpretation of Scripture is central to any argument favoring the liberationist elements in Wesley's economics. For Wesley, the holding of common property was not first a concept rooted in *political theory* (as it would be for Marx years later), but rather a concept taught in *Scripture* and exemplified among the early disciples. Wesley's challenge to private property among Christians was rooted in two fundamental theological convictions: First, all property ultimately belongs to God. Therefore, Christians are stewards, not owners, of what they possess. Second, Wesley believed that outward actions always flow from what he called the "tempers." When Christ transforms the tempers of an individual through the process of sanctification, the natural outworking of perfect love within her heart will necessitate the generous sharing of her property for the benefit of others. Thus, Wesley did not advocate a system of forced redistribution through taxes, but did insist that the holding of common property ought to be the normative practice among all true believers who steward God's resources properly and whose tempers are transformed by the Holy Spirit. Such economic themes are repeatedly emphasized throughout Wesley's sermons. See Wesley, "Sermon 50: The Use of Money," in *Works*, 2:263–80; "Sermon 51: The Good Steward," in *Works*, 2:281–91; "Sermon 131: The Danger of Increasing Riches," in *Works*, 4:177–86; "Sermon 87: The Danger of Riches," in *Works*, 3:227–46; "Sermon 115: Dives and Lazarus," in *Works*, 4:4–18; "Sermon 129: Heavenly Treasures in Earthen Vessels," in *Works*, 4:161–67; "Sermon 108: On Riches," in *Works*, 3:518–28, "Sermon 28: Upon our Lord's Sermon on the Mount, Discourse VIII," in *Works*, 1:612–31; and elsewhere.

Reacting to Jennings' interpretation of Wesley, Theodore R. Weber offered a rejoinder in 2001 in his *Politics in the Order of Salvation: Transforming Wesleyan Political Ethics,* the most exhaustive and thoroughly researched treatment of Wesley's political theology to date. Weber describes Wesley as an "organic constitutionalist" for whom loyalty to God, church, and country remain inextricably interwoven. In support, Weber quotes Wesley, who in 1747 wrote:

> Above all, mark that man who talks of loving the Church, and does not love the King. If he does not love the King, he cannot love God. And if he does not love God, he cannot love the Church. He loves the Church and King just alike. For indeed he loves neither one nor the other.[19]

Weber does not fully retreat to the hard line on Wesley's Tory values common among scholars in the first half of the twentieth century, but he does criticize modern scholars for contorting Wesley to fit their own agendas: "No aggressive investigation, no artful revisionism can overcome the fact that Wesley denied a political role to the people, and that he never wavered from this conviction."[20] Wesley was, according to Weber, unabashedly antidemocratic and antirepublican due to his unyielding loyalty to monarchism, albeit a limited, constitutional monarchism. In short, Weber accuses scholars of trying to fit Wesley into their own political agenda rather than taking his writings at face value.

In his argument portraying Wesley as an organic constitutionalist, Weber seeks to show that Wesley stands in "a conservative tradition, but it is not the conservatism of autocracy and absolutism. Rather, it is a tradition that respects established institutions that protect the values of people, while at the same time leaving the way open for change and improvement."[21] Weber does this by closely examining three crucial moments in the life of John Wesley's political formation: 1) the Jacobite rebellion of 1745, 2) the social upheaval and constitutional crisis caused by John Wilkes

19. John Wesley, "A Word to a Freeholder (1747)," in *Works*, 11:197–98, quoted in Weber, *Politics in the Order of Salvation*, 30–31.

20. Weber, *Politics in the Order of Salvation*, 32.

21. Ibid., 31.

and his followers in the 1760s, and 3) the division of the English empire during the American colonial rebellion. In each of these three events, Weber argues, John Wesley defended the established order and sought to distance himself from any perceived or genuine threat to the British king and system of government. Throughout all three of these crisis moments in English history, Wesley "trumpeted the virtues of the existing system and projected disaster if it were destroyed and replaced; and he attacked the radical (liberal) ideology with its arguments for natural rights, popular sovereignty, and social contract."[22]

While Weber faults scholars like Hynson and Jennings for distorting Wesley's actual political position, he does share their desire to redeem Wesley's thought for our contemporary context by articulating a genuinely Wesleyan political theology. In the final chapter of his book, Weber critiques Wesley for failing to connect his political theology to the transformationist elements of his soteriology. Wesley championed the idea of a threefold image of God in every human being: the natural image, the moral image, and the political image.[23] Yet of the three aspects in this typology, the least developed in Wesley's theology is the political image. Weber suggests that if Wesley were to extrapolate practical theology from his concept of the political image to the same extent that he did of the moral image, it would have led him to a deeper appreciation of human liberty and natural rights. In short, Weber argues that the political image of God can serve as a theological foundation for democratic, popular governance over and against the hierarchical top-down model of authority that Wesley inherited and defended. Thus, later Methodists can find lying dormant within Wesley's

22. Ibid., 110.

23. According to Wesley's anthropology, each of these three "images" remained intact subsequent to the fall of mankind. By "natural image," Wesley referred to the understanding, free will, and liberty imprinted on every human by the grace of God. By "moral image," Wesley meant knowledge of God's moral laws, to which God required perfect obedience. The "political image" refers to the Adamic relationship with the rest of creation as its steward and caretaker (Bryant, "Original Sin," 522–39). See also Wesley, "Sermon 44: Original Sin," in *Works*, 2:172–85.

own soteriology a strong case for the right of all people to govern themselves. This does not necessarily imply an endorsement of a particular form of government, according to Weber, but it does call into question Wesley's own strongly monarchical political persuasion.[24] We shall return to this important thesis and examine it in more depth in chapter 3.

From this overview of three scholars—Hynson, Jennings, and Weber—we can surmise that John Wesley was a complex character whose political, social, and economic theology is not easily distilled. Now we must turn our attention to what accounts for this wide variety in interpretations.

ACCOUNTING FOR THE VARIATIONS

Why have attempts to interpret the political and social theology of John Wesley generated such starkly divergent interpretations? As we have seen from our survey of the three scholars above, readings of Wesley range from depictions of him as a high church, pro-monarchy Tory to an advocate for democratic and republican values to a proto-Marxist liberation theologian. In this second section of the chapter, I will suggest three important distinctions that must be made in order to properly understand Wesley's political theology: 1) the distinction between his politics and his economics, 2) the distinction between Wesley's message to the Methodists and his message to society at large, and 3) the distinction between the young and the mature Wesley.

First, a strong differentiation needs to be maintained between Wesley's economic views and his political views. Obviously, politics and economics have always been intertwined with one another, but in Wesley's thought, this distinction must be maintained for the sake of clarity. In short, Wesley's economics, rooted in his reading of the New Testament, challenged the emerging capitalist ethos that was increasingly prevalent in his eighteenth-century British

24. For the full development of this argument, see especially chapter 12, "Recovering the Political Image of God," in Weber, *Politics in the Order of Salvation*, 391–420.

context. Indeed, at times, Wesley even called the very foundations of capitalism into question. In this sense then, Wesley harkened back to what Madron calls a form of "primitive communism."[25] Taken in the context of his own day, Wesley's economics could, in one sense, be described as conservative or traditionalist since they questioned the basic tenants of the newly emerging capitalist system and championed a return to biblical models of economic life. However, given the hegemony of *laissez-faire* free market-based economies in our own day, Wesley's economic theory could now be rightly called prophetically progressive inasmuch as he remained remarkably wary of the dangers inherent in any economic system that prizes individualism and the accumulation of private property above all else.[26]

Wesley's politics, on the other hand, remained committed to conservative Tory values throughout his life, and especially to the English constitution set down in 1689. Rooted in the deep conviction that all authority derives from God, Wesley remained suspicious about democratic forms of government and the right of people to choose their own leaders. Since Wesley's politics and economics are so different, it is therefore crucial for all interpreters to maintain a clear distinction between the two. Whereas Wesley's politics may leave modern readers committed to liberal democracy and the right of the people for self-governance unsatisfied, his economic theories certainly offer profound and important insights for contemporary politics. To emphasize the importance of this distinction, we will briefly take a look at each, beginning with a sketch of Wesley's economic ethics.

Repeatedly throughout his life, Wesley demonstrated his willingness to radically question the economic structures of his day. Randy Maddox offers a helpful summary of Wesley's economic ethics in four concise points:

---

25. Madron, "John Wesley on Economics," 108. See also my n. 18.

26. Some of Wesley's statements regarding the abuses of wealth bear an uncanny resemblance to recent statements made by Pope Francis that have challenged the idol of acquisitiveness.

(1) Ultimately everything belongs to God; (2) resources are placed in our care to use as God sees fit; (3) God desires that we use these resources to meet our necessities (i.e., providing food and shelter for ourselves and dependents), and then to help others in need; thus (4) spending resources on luxuries for ourselves while others remain in need is robbing God![27]

In the context of eighteenth-century England, where the economic thought of Adam Smith and John Locke increasingly impacted both government policies and popular opinion, Wesley promoted a counter-cultural alternative that took the early church as its prototype, and he attempted to recapture the Christian tradition of communality that had largely been lost by the time of the Enlightenment.

The language of "stewardship" is the most pervasive motif throughout Wesley's sermons, letters, and other scripts regarding Christian economic ethics. Since God is the Creator and Sustainer of all that exists, human beings never actually *own* anything. Rather, humans are entrusted with the property of God to be used for his purposes. Furthermore, since the basic law of Christian ethics is to love God and love our neighbors, Wesley believed all excess money must be utilized to promote the common good. Marquardt summarizes the centrality of both the concept of stewardship and the love commandment in Wesley's economic teachings:

According to Wesley, the purpose of earning and thrift is to make life's necessities available to all and to ameliorate or eliminate the distress of others. Doing so fulfills the commandment to love one's neighbor, and above all demonstrates obedience to the will of God, the owner. All persons must account before their Creator and Judge for what they have done with their money and all other goods entrusted to them and must receive God's reward or punishment.[28]

---

27. Maddox, *Responsible Grace*, 244.

28. Marquardt, *John Wesley's Social Ethics*, 37.

"Portrait of John Wesley" by Frank O. Salisbury, courtesy of the Marston Memorial Historical Archives.

Given his critique of private property rooted in a theological commitment to the love commandment and principle of steward-ship, Wesley offered harsh words of warning against the accumula-tion of wealth or expenditure of resources on needless luxuries. This theme appeared more frequently in Wesley's later ministry as he witnessed many Methodists increasing in riches and yet failing to properly steward their money for the use of the common good. Two years before his death, Wesley declared,

But why is self-denial in general so little practised [*sic*] at present among the Methodists? Why is so exceeding little of it to be found even in the oldest and largest societies? . . . The Methodists grow more and more self-indulgent, because they grow rich. Although many of them are still deplorably poor . . . yet many others, in the space of twenty, thirty, or forty years, are twenty, thirty, or yea a hundred times richer than they were when they first entered the society. And it is an observation which admits of few exceptions, that nine in ten of these decreased in grace in the same proportion as they increased in wealth. Indeed, according to the natural tendency of riches, we cannot expect it to be otherwise.[29]

Indeed, Wesley perceived the gradual accumulation of wealth to be one of the greatest threats to the future of the Methodist movement, since it entailed a rejection of both the love commandment and the acknowledgment of God's ownership over all of creation. A century later B. T. Roberts, as we will discuss in the next chapter, shared many of the same concerns, believing that extravagant riches were morally corroding the soul of the Methodist Episcopal churches in which he preached.

Thus, in his economics, Wesley defended the historic Christian values of charity and hospitality in an age of increasing individualism. He resisted the impulse common among many of his day (and ours!) to separate economic theory from the ethics of the Christian life. Vying against the emerging ethos of capitalism, Wesley proved himself willing time and again to shun the economic climate of eighteenth-century England and insist that a profound concern for the common good must take precedent in any proper Christian ethic. This leads Maddox to proclaim, "While Adam Smith held that surplus accumulation was the foundation of economic well-being, Wesley viewed it as a mortal sin!"[30]

While his stance against the presuppositions and abuses of capitalism set him apart from most of his contemporaries, in

29. Wesley, "Sermon 122: Causes of the Inefficacy of Christianity," in *Works*, 4:95, §16.

30. Maddox, *Responsible Grace*, 244–45.

contrast, Wesley's political views were much more mainstream. Eighteenth-century England was deeply divided between the Tories and Whigs.[31] Given this reality, Wesley sided with the Tories, vigorously challenging Whiggish politics and principles. Wesley feared the influence of the Whigs because he believed that their political philosophy denied the biblical teaching that authority comes from God, and he feared that this could ultimately lead to anarchy. As we have already noted, Wesley stood for stability, continuity, and order during the political upheavals of his day, almost without exception choosing to side with the British monarch. So deeply ingrained was Wesley's loyalty to his king and country that in 1756 he even offered to recruit soldiers for service in the king's army! Wesley wrote in a letter dated March 1 of that year that he was willing "to raise for His Majesty's service at least two hundred volunteers, to be supported by contributions among themselves; and to be ready in case of an invasion for a year (if needed so long) at His Majesty's pleasure."[32] Other evidence for Wesley's conservative political stance has already been cited in the overview of Weber's book, so it is not necessary to repeat that here.

Thus, there was a notable difference between Wesley's economics and his politics. In the former, Wesley is the prophet, standing at the margins of society and challenging its basic presuppositions and structure. In the latter, Wesley serves as a chaplain to the Tory Party, defending the political structures as they currently stand against what he perceived to be radical elements that could potentially cause upheaval and disorder. It is little wonder that

---

31. Weber explains the divided political climate within which Wesley was born and raised: "English political sentiment polarized around two alternative modes of representation as the form that English society should take for action in history. Tories supported the notion of the monarch ruling by divine indefeasible hereditary right—above the law because he or she was the source of the law, answerable to no one but God, due to passive obedience and nonresistance from all subjects . . . [Whereas] Whigs supported the concept of a government of king and Parliament together, with predominance of power on the parliamentary side" (Weber, *Politics in the Order of Salvation*, 162).

32. Quoted in Hosman, "Problem of Church and State," 237.

interpreters of Wesley today wrestle with these two very different portraits of his character.

In this sense, Theodore Jennings and Theodore Weber are talking past one another. Jennings emphasizes Wesley's economics since his agenda is to portray Wesley as a forefather to modern liberation theologians. Weber, on the other hand, focuses on Wesley's politics, leading him to a vision of Wesley as a man who never recognized the political implications of his own theology. Or, more precisely, Jennings finds resonances between Wesley's defense of traditional biblical economics and modern theologies of liberation. Weber, on the other hand, argues that very little resonance can be found between Wesley's political commitment to a constitutional monarch and the values of liberal democracy embraced by modern Europe and North America.

A second important distinction to make in the study of Wesley's political theology concerns the audience to whom Wesley addressed his social ethic. Jennings argues that Wesley concerned himself with advocating for the poor by pressing for changes in government policies.[33] But were Wesley's social ethics directed at politicians *or* at the classes, bands, and societies of Methodists? Related to this, did Wesley understand the systematic and structural nature of poverty, or did he view the transformation of individuals as the primary locus for addressing issues of economic injustice?

---

33. Jennings disagrees with the prevailing view that Wesley saw no role for government in the alleviation of poverty. He writes, "It simply is not the case that Wesley has nothing to say about the relation of poverty to government policy. Indeed it is precisely by way of his very solidarity with the poor and consequent awareness of their plight that the way is opened for Wesley to propose for government economic policy the same criterion he had found himself applying to the work of the Methodist movement," and in support, Jennings cites Wesley's *Thoughts on the Present Scarcity of Provisions* (Jennings, *Good News for the Poor*, 66–69).

This is perhaps pushing Wesley too far into the area of direct political involvement. Fundamentally, Wesley was concerned with the renewal of the *church* (that is, his beloved Church of England). A renewed church would then become effective in renewing the nation-state. Thus, Wesley's advocacy for change in governmental policy was generally indirect rather than direct.

To be sure, the majority of Wesley's political theology found in his sermons and other writing is not directed toward the government, but at the Methodist laity. For example, Wesley's well-known instruction to gain all you can, save all you can, and give all you can in his sermon "The Use of Money" was directed neither at the whole of society nor at government leaders, but only at committed Methodists.[34] Thus, the aforementioned convictions Wesley held about common property certainly do not imply that Wesley can be anachronistically dubbed a politically convinced communist or socialist. Rather, he perceived the holding of common property to be a normative ethic *within the church*. This explains why Wesley attempted to implement his economic ideals only within the parameters of the select societies.[35]

Furthermore, Wesley believed that the ultimate solution to societal ills was found within the transformation of *individual human hearts* by the grace of God working to undo the marks of original sin. For example, when Wesley spoke of the evils of war, he never offered a statement about war's systemic causes, but rather blamed war's existence upon the fallen nature of individual human beings.[36] In the same way, Wesley's many appeals advocating generosity to the poor remained largely on the level of personal charity; with a few notable exceptions to be examined later, any calls for the creation of progressive taxation or governmental welfare systems remain absent from Wesley's sermons and writing.[37]

34. Wesley, "The Use of Money," in *Works*, 2:263–80.

35. Maddox, "Visit the Poor," 41.

36. Weber, *Politics in the Order of Salvation*, 362.

37. See again, ibid., "The Use of Money," in *Works*, 2:263–80. One notable exception to this, however, is Wesley's "Thoughts on the Present Scarcity of Provisions" in which Wesley *does* call upon the government to make specific changes in policy in order to address the plight of the extremely poor. Specifically, Wesley calls for the prohibition of the distillation of hard liquors, a heavy tax on luxury goods, a reduction in the size of farms, limitations on excessive luxury, and an effort to pay off the national debt. See John Wesley, "Thoughts on the Present Scarcity of Provisions (1773)," in *Works of John Wesley*, 11:58–59; hereafter referred to as *Works (Jackson)*. Wesley's opposition to the slave trade is a second notable exception. These exceptions are so important that they will be discussed in greater detail later.

Maddox notes that even during the most politically active years of Wesley's life, "political advocacy was hardly [Wesley's] dominant concern. Wesley published many more sermons in his last years encouraging his Methodist followers to share their resources voluntarily with others in need than he did tracts calling for the political reform of social and economic structures."[38]

Nevertheless, an argument can be made that any expectation of Wesley to be aware of the systemic, political causes of poverty would be unfairly anachronistic. Wesley was a product of his own time—a time deeply committed to Enlightenment individualism and, in comparison to today, largely unaware of the systemic causes of poverty. Given this context, it is truly remarkable that Wesley, especially in the later years of his life, did in fact recognize some of the structural causes of poverty.[39] The German Wesley scholar Manfred Marquardt, for example, argues that even though Wesley had a limited awareness of the structural causes of society's ills (due to his historical location), his soteriology does provide a foundation and trajectory for a social ethic that addresses social ills on the systematic level. Indeed, Marquardt goes beyond this and, citing Wesley's "Thoughts on the Present Scarcity of Provisions," concludes,

> For Wesley, the king's task was therefore to use his power of taxation to more equitably distribute goods and to eliminate grave distresses, to provide food and employment for people . . . He regarded a number of governmental interventions as essential to achieving lower [food] prices, and he perceived the national government and Parliament as the appropriate agencies [to accomplish this].[40]

As already mentioned, the two most obvious examples of Wesley's willingness to engage in political advocacy on the systemic

38. Maddox, "Nurturing the New Creation," 34.

39. For an examination of the changes in Wesley's eschatology in the final two decades of his life and the socioeconomic implications of this shift, see ibid., 21–52.

40. Marquardt, *John Wesley's Social Ethics*, 46–47.

level can be found in his opposition to the slave trade and in his "Thoughts on the Present Scarcity of Provisions," written in 1773. Because these two aspects of Wesley's thought are so crucial for understanding his political theology, it is appropriate to examine them in more detail.

Wesley's willingness to oppose the status quo of society on a structural level is most clearly expressed in his vocal opposition to slavery and, particularly, the *trade* of slaves that many merchants in his nation profited from. Wesley described slavery as "that execrable sum of all villanies" in a letter to William Wilberforce written at the end of his life.[41] But the Anglican state church to which Wesley belonged generally tolerated the slave trade without objection. The few clergy in the first half of the eighteenth century who did vocally oppose the practice were largely ignored. Although there are indications that he disapproved of slavery and the treatment of blacks in his early years,[42] Wesley finally publicly announced his opposition in 1774 with his tract, *Thoughts upon Slavery*. In his argument that British ships ought to cease participating in the slave trade, Wesley appeals to both biblical theology and natural law. Adopting the common political rhetoric of the Enlightenment, Wesley interprets the issue of slavery to be fundamentally about human rights: "Better no trade, than trade procured by villainy. It is far better to have no wealth than to gain wealth at the expense of virtue. Better is honest poverty, than all the riches bought by the tears, and sweat, and blood, of our fellow-creatures."[43]

Thus, despite the laws and common practices of his nation that condoned the slave trade, Wesley critiqued British law and questioned the governing authorities who created them. To those who countered Wesley by arguing that slavery was perfectly legal, Wesley replied,

41. Wesley, Letter to William Wilberforce, February 24, 1791, in *Letters*, 8:264–65.

42. Despite the objections of whites, Wesley baptized and administered the Lord's Supper to blacks and whites alike during his visit to the colonies in the 1730s. See Marquardt, *John Wesley's Social Ethics*, 71.

43. Wesley, *Works (Jackson)*, 11:74.

> But can law, human law, change the nature of things? Can it turn darkness into light, or evil into good? By no means! Notwithstanding ten thousand laws, right is right, and wrong is wrong still. There must still remain an essential difference between justice and injustice, cruelty and mercy.[44]

Wesley proves through his opposition to the slave trade that he stands in that precarious space between Rom 13 and Rev 13: between submission to God-ordained authority and the recognition that the governmental principalities and powers can themselves become demonic. Theodore Jennings comments, "Here Wesley, who on so many occasions must appeal to the appropriateness of obeying the law, breaks out into a clear statement of the relativity of all laws, the necessity of obeying the dictates of mercy and justice before any law."[45] For Wesley, therefore, submission and passive obedience to authority were not absolutes. And in his vocal opposition to slavery, we find a prime example of Wesley's willingness to engage in advocacy not only on the level of the individual, but also in seeking political and structural change.

Slavery was not, however, the only issue that compelled Wesley to critique the laws of his nation. As mentioned earlier, he also proved willing to oppose economic policies that exacerbated the plight of the poor. When Wesley writes his "Thoughts on the Present Scarcity of Provisions," in which he chastises an economic structure that allows some to live in luxury while others starve, he argues that much of the blame for the extreme poverty and hunger in England can be lain at the feet of those who distill spirituous liquors, a practice which requires inordinate amounts of wheat and grain. He also blamed the "monopolizing of farms," the "enormous taxes, which are laid on almost everything that can be named," and the obsession of the rich with needless luxuries.[46]

The suggestions that Wesley offers for solving the problem of poverty are revealing. He calls upon the government to reduce

44. Ibid., 11:70.
45. Jennings, *Good News to the Poor*, 84.
46. Wesley, *Works (Jackson)*, 11:53–59.

the price of basic foods, limit the distillation of liquor, lay a heavy tax on the wealthy and on the luxury goods they purchase, decrease the size of farms (through breaking up monopolies), and "repress . . . luxury; whether by laws, by example, or by both."[47] Thus, Wesley's concern for alleviating extreme poverty and hunger compelled him to engage in open, public criticism of government policy. With these notable exceptions in mind, then, we may conclude that for Wesley, the solution to economic injustice may in certain instances involve *both* addressing the needs of the individual *and* the reshaping of laws and public policy.[48]

Yet despite these two examples of Wesley's willingness to engage in the political sphere, it must be acknowledged that for most of his life, Wesley remained reticent about pursuing socioeconomic reform by appealing to the government. Randy Maddox outlines three possible explanations for this reticence that have been offered by various scholars: 1) The conservative political values that Wesley inherited from his parents led him to distrust political revolutionaries seeking radical change to the socioeconomic order, 2) Wesley held a deep-seated pessimism about the prospect of social change due to his "bourgeois status," and 3) Wesley rarely addressed the political arena, especially prior to the 1770s, because of how small and politically insignificant his movement was within the culture at large.[49]

A third and final distinction that must be maintained in the study of John Wesley's political theology is the difference between Wesley's thought in his early years from that of his later years.

47. Ibid., 11:58.

48. Though this work is focused on the latter, ample evidence in John Wesley's writings can be cited for the former. Wesley did believe that spiritual revival in each individual human heart would ultimately transform society and produce greater economic equality. In this sense, Wesley engages in what Graham Ward calls "macropolitics" *and* "micropolitics." See Ward, *The Politics of Discipleship*, 28–32. In today's context, when many Christians argue for either one or the other, it is refreshing to find in Wesley an example of concern for *both* personal piety and social justice.

49. Maddox, "Nurturing the New Creation," 34. Maddox goes on to consider the role Wesley's millennial eschatology played in his convictions about God's work to bring in a new creation.

Hynson's work has proven helpful for subsequent scholars who notice the shifting nature of Wesley's political theology. Although Jason Vickers critiques Hynson for offering a two-stage theory that is overly simplistic and for failing to properly account for the shifting political landscape of eighteenth-century England,[50] the historian must acknowledge that the most politically active years of John Wesley's life were his final two decades. Throughout the 1770s and onward Wesley proved increasingly willing to challenge the status quo. Is it fair to note, then, that Wesley's life does provide a *trajectory* that points toward political engagement[51]—lobbying in the political sphere on behalf of the poor, critiquing structural issues which exacerbate class distinctions, and advocating for greater human liberty? Asking where John Wesley would locate himself in today's political landscape is certainly a legitimate question for modern theologians.

Interpreting the political and social ethics of John Wesley continues to be a crucial task for theologians seeking to bring the founder of Methodism into conversation with the church today. Of course, any Wesleyan political theology must use John Wesley as its starting place, but this does not necessarily entail that Wesley must be given the last word. As we have seen, Wesley's own life sets a *trajectory* in a particular direction—toward an increasing conviction of the freedom and agency of individuals in the political process, a growing willingness to critique abuses of power, and a burgeoning hopefulness about the work of social reform within God's narrative of salvation. In a sense, then, the important question for today's political theologian within the Wesleyan tradition is not merely "What did Wesley think?" but rather "What would Wesley think now?" and "Toward what end does the trajectory of

---

50. Vickers, *Wesley: A Guide for the Perplexed*, 68–71. Vickers maintains that Wesley's political loyalties shifted very little over his lifetime, but that the Tory party itself was what changed and that Wesley was carried along with it.

51. I am not here arguing for specific, identifiable pivots in Wesley's political thinking or even for distinct "stages" during his lifetime, as Weber does, but more humbly that a definite trajectory can be perceived within Wesley's life toward increased recognition that it is a Christian's duty to engage social structures on the political level.

Wesley's theology point?" B. T. Roberts represents one example of a church leader who sought to remain faithful to the Wesleyan vision while also adapting it into his own context. And so, at this point, we move forward a century and across an ocean to continue the quest for a robust Wesleyan political theology.

2

B. T. Roberts, Populist and Wesleyan

IN THE HISTORY OF American Methodism, Benjamin Titus Roberts is most well known as the founder of the Free Methodist Church. Having been expelled by the Methodist Episcopal Church at the Genesee Annual Conference in 1858 for "unchristian and immoral conduct,"[1] Roberts and several other expelled clergy organized the Free Methodist Church two years later in 1860. Although that story has been recounted in many volumes,[2] much lesser known is the story of B. T. Roberts' political activism and involvement with the early Populist movement in the late nineteenth century. The purpose of this chapter is to recount this less familiar story, and in the process, to examine the theologically grounded political and economic thought of B. T. Roberts that led him to become so involved in the Populist movement. In the end I hope to demonstrate

---

1. Roberts, *Why Another Sect*, 71. Roberts denies these charges and maintains that he was expelled for preaching sermons and publishing articles that maintained the biblical standard of holiness and articulated John Wesley's doctrine of entire sanctification. According to the early Free Methodists, Roberts and his fellow "Nazarite" reform party were expelled for criticizing the larger Methodist church for abandoning these teachings.

2. See most famously Hogue, *History of the Free Methodist Church*; Marston, *From Age to Age*; and Snyder, *Populist Saints*.

that Roberts' political activism emerged from his underlying theological convictions—convictions that are distinctively Wesleyan.

This chapter will be divided into three sections. First, in order to explore the context of Roberts' day, I will offer a brief introduction to populism as it emerged in late nineteenth-century rural America. Second, I will note B. T. Roberts' involvement in the movement, particularly as an organizer of farmers in his native New York state. Third, I will assess the theological convictions that informed Roberts' political activism, suggesting that specifically his reading of Scripture, his soteriology, and his eschatology underpinned his Populist efforts.

POPULISM IN LATE NINETEENTH-CENTURY AMERICA

In the final three decades of the nineteenth century, America witnessed dramatic economic and social changes. In 1877, for example, President Rutherford B. Hayes signaled his intention to no longer use federal troops as protection for the civil rights of African-Americans in the South. That same year, prompted by the increasing power of the railroad industry and the growing income gap between owners and laborers, the railroad workers instigated the Great Strike of 1877, which paralyzed much of the nation's railroad system. This event awakened the nation to the class tensions that had been simmering for some time. Spurred on by what had been the nation's worst depression to date—what is now known as the "Long Depression" during the years between 1873 and 1896—alliances coalesced among the rural poor, who distrusted the increasing power and influence of large corporations concentrated in the cities.[3] These rapid changes, exacerbated by rapid industrialization and urbanization, provided a seedbed of unrest for what would eventually germinate as the Populist movement.

Of the many people and groups negatively impacted by the Long Depression, farmers were perhaps the hardest hit. The

---

3. McMath, *American Populism*, 3–4.

well-known historian Howard Zinn paints a picture of the economic pressures farmers faced during the last quarter of the nineteenth century, precipitating the rise of the Populist movement:

> Land cost money, and machines cost money—so farmers had to borrow, hoping that the prices of their harvests would stay high so they could pay back the bank for the loan, the railroad for transportation, the grain merchant for handling their grain, the storage elevator for storing it. But they found the prices for their produce going down, and the prices of transportation and loans going up, because the individual farmer could not control the price of his grain, while the monopolist railroad and the monopolist banker could charge what they liked.[4]

Historians disagree about where precisely to pinpoint the beginning of the Populist movement, likely as the result of its decentralized and amorphous character. Charles Postel, author of *The Populist Vision*, begins his narrative in "the dust and smoke of the central Texas frontier,"[5] but other historians locate Populist beginnings among black farmers in the South, still others within the agrarian regions of central and western New York, and still others elsewhere.[6] Most likely, however, populism emerged concurrently within all of these regions, and among differing groups motivated by their desperate economic conditions.

The difficulty of properly defining the Populist movement lies in the fact that its history long precedes the actual creation of a political party. And even when the so-called official Populist Party of the 1890s emerged, it was less a typically structured political party

---

4. Zinn, *People's History*, 283.

5. Postel, *Populist Vision*, 25.

6. Robert McMath argues in his social history of the movement that New York is the proper originating locus for the movement. Lee Benson concurs, stating that the Farmers' Alliance generated the Populist movement and that the alliance began in New York and emanated from there to the rest of the country (Snyder, *Populist Saints*, 751). John Hicks argues that the movement began among wheat farmers in the upper Midwest, and C. Vann Woodward locates it in the southern Cotton Belt. See McMath, *American Populism*; Hicks, *Populist Revolt*; Woodward, *Origins of the New South*.

than "a coalition of reform organizations."[7] The coalition that met in Cincinnati in 1891, for example, joined together the following organizations: The Farmers' Alliance and Industrial Union, the National Farmers' Alliance, the Colored Farmers' Alliance, the Farmers' Mutual Benefit Association, the Knights of Labor, the Women's Alliance, the Citizens' Alliance, and other reform groups.[8] Thus, from its beginnings, the Populist movement emerged from grassroots efforts and was localized rather than centralized.

The earliest iterations of the movement sought to remain nonpartisan and chose instead to act merely as catalysts for reform within the already established political parties. Before the Populists coalesced, a consortium of farmers known as "grangers" organized to effect public policy. Due to their petitions and advocacy, the Granger Movement witnessed laws passed to ease the pressure placed on farmers in numerous states, yet their gains were minimal.[9] Progress was too slow for the masses of desperate farmers, so when gradual reform through lobbying proved to be only nominally effective at eliciting structural change, the Populists became more overtly political, eventually nominating their own candidates for national office.

What was the agenda of the Populists? In 1886 the Farmers' Alliance in Texas created the first document of the Populist movement called the "Cleburne Demands," which asked for the creation of "such legislation as shall secure to our people freedom from the onerous and shameful abuses that the industrial classes are now suffering at the hands of arrogant capitalists and powerful organizations."[10] Central to the movement was a deep suspicion of the newly emerging corporate class, composed of powerful business owners who wielded considerable political influence. As a result, the Populists became widely known for opposing monopolies, abusive railroad pricing, inequitable banking policies, government

7. Postel, *Populist Vision*, 12.

8. Ibid.

9. For examples of the legislation proposed and passed by the Grangers, see Buck, *Granger Movement*, 102–22.

10. Quoted in Zinn, *People's History*, 286.

corruption, and the growing income gap.[11] These concerns united an otherwise diverse group of people into a common cause.

In the five years between 1887 and 1892 the Farmers' Alliance grew from two hundred thousand members to over two million farm families in forty-three different states. The movement organized journals and newspapers to spread the message, cooperative insurance programs to protect farmers from years of famine, boycotts against price gougers, and eventually the election of thirty-eight Alliance members to Congress in 1890.[12] The historian Lawrence Goodwyn called it "the most massive organizing drive by any citizen institution of nineteenth-century America."[13] And in the South, the common interests of white and black Populists amalgamated to such a degree that one historian commented, "Never before or since have the two races in the South come so closer together as they did during the Populist struggles."[14]

Nevertheless, no sooner did this vast movement congeal to form an official political party, known as the People's Party (or the Populist Party), than it suffered defeat in the election of 1896 by allying itself to the Democratic Party and its candidate William Jennings Bryan. After Bryan's defeat, the Populist movement dissipated into the folds of the larger Democratic Party. Howard Zinn attributes the demise of the movement to its alliance with electoral politics, which proved fatal since "electoral politics brought into the top leadership the political brokers instead of the agrarian radicals."[15] According to many historical interpreters, the movement's decision to abandon its grassroots origins in favor of political legitimacy proved to be its downfall.

Despite its short-lived formal existence as a third-party option in American politics, the ideals and values of populism live on to this day. A suspicion of concentrated political power and influence, a critique of the extremes of unfettered capitalism, concerns

11. Postel, *Populist Vision*, 11.

12. Zinn, *People's History*, 286–87.

13. Goodwyn, *Populist Moment*, 56.

14. Woodward, quoted in Zinn, *People's History*, 292.

15. Zinn, *People's History*, 294.

about the growing income gap, and the demands for greater regulation of the financial industry all represent echoes in our own day of populism. In the century following the downfall of populism, America did adopt many of populism's ideas and values. The residuum of populism includes the Federal Reserve Act of 1913, the graduated income tax, and Theodore Roosevelt's "trust busting" efforts. (Some would even include Franklin Roosevelt's New Deal and Lyndon Johnson's Great Society in this list). Reflecting on this legacy, Populist scholar Charles Postel claims, "By a turn of fate, populism proved far more successful dead than alive."[16] Recently, some have even suggested that *both* the Occupy Wall Street Movement and the Tea Party Movement can be interpreted as direct descendants of the populism of the late nineteenth century since both are deeply suspicious of consolidated power.[17] Undoubtedly, the spirit of populism, which perpetually aims "to reshape government as an agency of the majority rather than of the corporate and wealthy minority,"[18] lives on to this day in American politics.

B. T. ROBERTS AND THE FARMERS' ALLIANCE

Within such a politically volatile atmosphere, B. T. Roberts ministered to the needs of poor farmers, and having seen their need firsthand, was eventually moved to play a key role in the beginnings of the Populist movement. As previously mentioned, until recently little attention was given to Roberts' political activism and ideas. The Free Methodist Church, the denomination founded by Roberts, gradually drifted away from the populism of its founder, adopting a politically and socially conservative role in American culture,[19] and as a result, more research has been devoted to

16. Postel, *Populist Vision*, 271. For more on populism's legacy, see ibid., 269–89.

17. See, for example, Chinni, "Are Occupy Wall Street."

18. Postel, *Populist Vision*, 288.

19. For a fascinating social history of the Free Methodist movement that examines the shifting theology and practice of the denomination through a close examination of the Free Methodist Book of Discipline, see Wall,

Roberts' views on entire sanctification and holiness than to his populism.[20] However, this changed in 2006 with the publication of Howard Snyder's massive 975-page biography of B. T. Roberts and his wife, Ellen. Here I will summarize Roberts' crucial involvement in the establishment of the Farmers' Alliance in New York, drawing especially from Snyder's research.

B. T. Roberts maintained a deep love for agriculture and farming throughout his life. Even during some of the busiest years of his ministry as a Free Methodist leader, Roberts found time to work the land as a part-time farmer. As a result, Roberts remained keenly aware of the problems and issues farmers faced during the economic crises that composed the Long Depression. He witnessed firsthand how the price gouging of the railroad industry, for example, prevented farmers in central and western New York from making a profit.[21] By the late nineteenth century, railroads had risen to a position of almost untouchable economic power, which negatively impacted community life in the rural northeast. Public sentiment gradually turned against the railroads as many began to call for increased public control of the industry.[22] Rooted in a deep biblical concern for justice, Roberts heard the cries of his fellow farmers and decided that they "must engage in political action to protect themselves from the growing railroad power. He

---

"Embourgeoisement," 117–29.

20. The other biographies of B. T. Roberts by his son Benson Roberts (published in 1900) and by Clarence Zahniser (published in 1957) each offer only passing references to Roberts' connection to populism (Snyder, *Populist Saints*, 751–52 n. 29).

21. Realizing the control they exerted over New York's farmers, the railroad industry engaged in price-fixing to maximize their profit. During the 1870s and 80s it was more expensive to ship crops to New York City from Rochester, NY, than it was to ship them from the grain fields of Iowa (Benson, *Merchants, Farmers, and Railroads*, 81). Benson further notes that the state of New York refused to regulate the railroad industry, adopting legislation in 1850 that he calls "perhaps the most sweeping legislative endorsement of *laissez-faire* [capitalism] in American history" (quoted in Snyder, *Populist Saints*, 749).

22. Ely, *Railroads and American Law*, 83.

proposed political action to control the railroads at a time when this idea was novel—not to say radical or abhorrent."[23]

Benjamin Titus Roberts,
courtesy of the Marston Memorial Historical Archives.

Roberts utilized the same networking and organizing skills that made him such a capable denominational leader to rally farmers for political engagement. In March of 1877, he authored a notice that appeared in the *Yates County Chronicle* of Penn Yan, New York, which read:

23. Snyder, *Populist Saints*, 746.

> In a country where laws are made and administered, of-
> ten according to popular clamor, men of class, if united,
> may exert a much more powerful influence than men of
> a much larger class, if acting in their individual character.
> Seeing this, all the great interests of the State, except the
> farming interest, have become thoroughly organized. As
> a result there is manifest a strong tendency, by our Leg-
> islature, to enact laws operating unjustly against farmers
> . . . We therefore call a convention of the farmers of this
> State, to meet . . . to effect a permanent organization of
> farmers of this State and such other business as the occa-
> sion may demand.[24]

In this revealing statement, we note first that Roberts adopted
language of class struggle critical of *laissez-faire* capitalism, which
would have been deemed un-American by some of Roberts' contemporaries. Secondly, Roberts' recognition that the economic
obstacles facing farmers were systemic in nature and needed to be
addressed through organized local, regional, and nationwide political action. Thirdly, we note that Roberts sought to unify farmers, a group of people naturally predisposed to value independence
and autonomy, into a single alliance for their mutual benefit. These
insights may seem rather obvious in our own day, but as Snyder
comments, they were radical and controversial within the culture
of self-reliance that pervaded rural nineteenth-century America.

Roberts spoke publicly at a meeting of the Western New
York Agricultural Society in 1872 and later turned his lecture
into a pamphlet entitled "Conspiracies Against Farmers." In it,
he blamed the plight of the farmers on unfair "grants to railroads
. . . the bonding system, and the system of National Banks." The
solution, Roberts argued, could only be found in organized political action devoted to overturning "these evils, under which the
country groans."[25] Sixteen months later Roberts wrote a letter to
the *New York Times*, which was published on the second page of
the newspaper under the title "Town Bonds for Railroads." In it he

24. "State Convention of Farmers," 2, quoted in Snyder, *Populist Saints*,
745.

25. Ibid., 753.

laments the present system in which townships as a whole can be bonded by railroads for the use of privately held property—a system Roberts describes as "a legalized plan for robbing farmers."[26] One month later, Roberts traveled to St. Louis to once more spread his message that farmers must unite into a national alliance.[27]

Thus, through his advocacy as a speaker, organizer, and author, Roberts played a crucial role in the fragile days of the infancy of the Farmers' Alliance. When the first Alliance organized locally in Rochester, New York, in March of 1875, Roberts played a key role in the deliberations.[28] This was the *first* formally organized Farmers' Alliance in the nation, and it stated its mission as follows:

> Its chief object was to effect legislation in the interest of the agriculturist, not by distinct party action, but through each political party to secure nominations and election of candidates pledged to support such just and equal laws as would bear on the interests of agriculture, also to secure equal representation of the farming class in the legislature of the State.[29]

Roberts later wrote a letter to a fellow leader in the alliance in which he claimed to be the originator of the Alliance, having first spread word of the meeting and framing the constitutions and bylaws that were eventually adopted by the alliance.[30]

Two years later the local chapter of the Farmers' Alliance established in Rochester would merge with other local chapters to form the New York State Farmers' Alliance, which would in turn become a key player in the larger nationwide Populist movement. Apparently, as the organization matured and grew in power and influence, Roberts took a less active role, choosing to focus his time on leading the Free Methodist Church.[31] Roberts never became a key leader of the movement during its late stages in the 1880s

26. Ibid.
27. Ibid., 754.
28. Ibid., 755.
29. Root, "Origins of the Farmer's Alliance," 1016.
30. Snyder, *Populist Saints*, 757 n. 53.
31. Ibid., 772.

and 90s, yet his influence on the organization of the movement in those fragile days of its infancy is undeniable.

Howard Snyder suggests four key ways in which Roberts' political efforts eventually bore fruit. First, the Alliance helped generate dramatically increased regulation of the railroad industry through the establishment of the New York Railroad Commission in 1882. Before that legislation, the industry had been almost entirely unregulated, resulting in many of the grievances held by New York farmers. Second, it proved that farmers could, in fact, wield important political influence if they united in a common effort. Furthermore, this influence did not depend on the establishment of an independent political party, but could instead be accomplished by lobbying the existing bipartisan system. Third, the Alliance directly led to the formation of the National Anti-Monopoly League. This important body, composed of such diverse groups as "merchant reformers, old-style 'Jefferson democrats,' labor leaders, Greenbackers, and socially conscious ministers," was formed to "support and defend the rights of the many as against the privileges of the few."[32] Finally and most importantly, the New York State Alliance, together with other alliances formed shortly after, ignited the nationwide movement of populism.[33]

THE THEOLOGICAL ROOTS OF B. T. ROBERTS' POPULISM

Having now both summarized the nature of the Populist movement and provided a brief history of B. T. Roberts' involvement in the early rise of the Farmers' Alliance, we are prepared to examine the theological foundation upon which Roberts based his political ideology, noting in particular their rootedness in John Wesley's thought. In what follows, I will first examine Roberts' particular concern for the poor, which, like Wesley's, developed from his

32. Benson, *Merchants, Farmers, and Railroads*, 150–51. For a closer examination of the legacy of the Anti-Monopoly League, see chapter 8 of Benson's book.

33. Ibid., 773–74.

reading of Scripture. Then I will examine both his soteriology and eschatology, arguing that these played an essential role in informing Roberts' political activism.

From its very beginning, the Free Methodist Church has been particularly devoted to ministry and evangelism among the poor. At its inception in 1860, the newly formed denomination articulated its mission as twofold: "to maintain the Bible standard of Christianity and to preach the gospel to the poor."[34] For Roberts, the theological foundation for this particular concern for the poor was located in Jesus' ministry as recorded in the gospels. Roberts, following in the footsteps of John Wesley, held a high view of Scripture and viewed it as the primary source for Christian doctrine and practice. In his book *Fishers of Men*, written to Free Methodist clergy as an exhortation for evangelism, Roberts explains his theological method:

> The effort has been to take no position that is not sustained by a fair interpretation of the Word of God. To this Word we bow with the most cordial submission. If our work may be thought by some to be radical, we beg them to bear in mind that the Bible is a radical book.[35]

And later, Roberts instructs his pastors:

> Preaching, to promote God's work, must be Scriptural. One plain text proves more than a dozen arguments. Logic can be met with logic, but from the Word of God there is no appeal.[36]

Therefore, when Roberts read in the Gospel of Luke that the hallmark of Jesus' ministry was to "preach the good news to the poor," he mandated that this be the normative practice for all Free Methodist ministers of the gospel.

Perhaps the best illustration of B. T. Roberts' desire to make the gospel available to the poor can be seen in the controversy over pew rental. Roberts, originally an ordained minister in the

---

34. Quoted in Kostlevy, "Benjamin Titus Roberts," 56.

35. Roberts, *Fishers of Men*, 7–8.

36. Ibid., 86.

Methodist Episcopal Church until his expulsion in 1858, objected strongly to the practice of pew rental, which had become a widespread method for raising funds in Methodist Episcopal churches during the mid-nineteenth century. In the 1850s Roberts' mother church removed wording from its *Book of Discipline* that forbade members from wearing "superfluous ornaments" and softened the language demanding that churches be built "plain and with free seats"—both rules that ensured Methodism's historic sensitivity and concern for the poor. Roberts believed that this shift unfairly discriminated against the poor and publicly demanded that the practice of pew rental be abolished. He wrote scathingly that charging people for the right to sit in church "is not of Christ. It has no warrant in the gospel. It cannot summon a single precept of the New Testament to its support . . . To the banquet Jesus has provided all are invited to come and eat without money and without price."[37] Roberts' critiques of the Methodist Episcopal Church certain echo Wesley's own words of warning about the danger that wealth posed to his growing Methodist movement.

Eventually, Roberts' vocal opposition to the practice of pew rental earned him the disfavor of his superiors in the Methodist Episcopal Church and was one factor contributing to his expulsion. Yet throughout the controversy, Roberts refused to compromise, convinced that his position alone was scripturally defensible. In an article published in the *Northern Christian Advocate* in 1856, Roberts insisted, "Several precepts of the Bible plainly require that the house of the Lord should be free for all who may wish to assemble there for purposes of worship" and that charging money for a place to sit does "great violence . . . to the Scriptures," amounting to a "perversion of the Divine record."[38] He found the practice to be particularly egregious because it introduced a class system into the church and communicated to the poor that they were unwelcome.

This controversy over pew rental provides just *one* example of the ethical centrality of ministry to the poor in Roberts' mind and the role that Scripture played in defending his position. In fact,

37. Roberts, "Renting Pews," *Earnest Christian*, June 1872, 190.
38. Quoted in Snyder, *Populist Saints*, 346.

Roberts advanced his advocacy for the poor to such an extent that at least one theologian has compared him to the Latin American liberation theologians who, over a century later, would place the poor at the center of their theological project, insisting on a divine "preferential option for the poor."[39] Given this concern, it was a natural development for Roberts to become politically involved in the Populist movement in his later years.

B. T. Robert's soteriology also provided a theological foundation for his populism. As a deeply committed Methodist seeking to return his beloved church to "earnest Christianity," Roberts believed in and preached the doctrine of entire sanctification. Roberts deliberately echoed the teachings of John Wesley by insisting that God desires his people to be made holy through the infilling of the Holy Spirit. This "peculiar doctrine" of Methodism insists that the process of sanctification culminates in a crisis moment of complete surrender to the will of God such that the Christian is inwardly cleansed of the guilt and power of sin and desires nothing but complete obedience to God's law. Entire sanctification, like justification, is a gracious gift of God given to those who seek it through faith. Roberts articulated his theology of entire sanctification, or what he elsewhere referred to as "perfect love," in his *Holiness Teachings*:

> Many appear to think that they can possess saving grace without any measure of holiness. This is a fundamental error. When God forgives, he says, with power, "Go, sin no more." Such a change is wrought, instantaneously, in the moral nature of one whom God forgives, that from that moment he has power over his sinful appetites and passions . . . From being a sinner he has become, in an important sense, a holy man . . . He is sanctified wholly.[40]

Roberts was certainly not unique in his insistence on adhering to entire sanctification as the goal of the Christian life. He stands within the larger holiness tradition and among other American preachers and theologians such as Charles Finney, Nathan

39. See Kostlevy, "Benjamin Titus Roberts," 51–67.

40. Roberts, *Holiness Teachings*, 138.

Bangs, and Phoebe Palmer, each of whom were concerned with promoting a similar message.[41] This confidence in the perfectibility of human nature emerged not only from their interpretation of Scripture, but also fit well within the context of the pervasive optimism of pre-Civil War nineteenth-century America.

Importantly for our purposes, this deep conviction that human nature may be perfected in this present life also shaped how Roberts, and other holiness theologians like him, viewed society at large. If God's grace can utterly vanquish sin in an individual human heart, what is to prevent God from transforming all of society as well? Following this line of thought, the revivalism of the holiness movement fed directly into crusades for social reform.[42] Holiness theology proved to be a catalyst for evangelical involvement in the abolition movement, and later, in the Populist and temperance movements.

Whereas twentieth-century evangelicalism frequently divorced the concerns for social justice and personal piety, Roberts and other leaders of the holiness movement believed the two to be inseparable. Salvation involved not only the inner transformation of the heart, but also the outer transformation of human interactions and relationships in community. Snyder describes Roberts' holistic soteriology thus: "Holiness extends to every area of life. Roberts opposed any split-level view that would put spirituality on one plane and business, politics, and economics on another."[43] He quotes Roberts as saying, "Business is not one thing and religion another. There is not a branch of holiness into which true religion does not enter and exert a controlling influence."[44]

---

41. For an examination of how Palmer and other American Methodists taught entire sanctification in the American context, see Noll, *America's God*, 359–62.

42. For more on the connection between nineteenth-century holiness theology and social reform movements, see Dayton, *Discovering an Evangelical Heritage*; Smith, *Revivalism and Social Reform*; and Magnuson, *Salvation in the Slums*.

43. Snyder, *Populist Saints*, 807.

44. Ibid., 807.

Thus, politics and economics were not amoral disciplines. Rather, the way a society organizes its economy, industry, and social structures reveals the extent to which they are either in accordance with or in opposition to the will of God. Roberts' holistic concern for both the souls *and bodies* of his parishioners led him to engage in political activism against an economic system that marginalized the people under his care. This is why Roberts, in his book *First Lessons on Money*, not only offers advice to individual families about how to make and save money, but also addresses larger structural issues such as the banking system and money supply.[45] Here Roberts is building on the foundation laid by Wesley, but using the tools available to him in his own day to expand upon the Wesleyan theological project.

Finally, Roberts' political commitments were not only informed by his special concern for the poor and his understanding of transformative power of salvation, but also by his eschatology. Beginning in the 1870s and carrying on into the twentieth century, the evangelicalism that originally grew out of the Second Great Awakening shifted to embrace premillennialism—the view that Christ's return would come very soon, removing the saints from the world in a moment of glorious "rapture." Prior to the Civil War, evangelical eschatology was primarily postmillennial, but the devastation caused by the Civil War had a profound impact on theologians, who became more pessimistic about the ability of human progress to bring about the kingdom of God.[46] Historian Donald Dayton describes the social and political implications of this shift from postmillennialism to premillennialism:

> But more characteristic was the tendency to abandon long-range social amelioration for a massive effort to preach the gospel to as many as possible before the return of Christ. The vision was now one of rescue from a fallen world. Just as Jesus was expected momentarily on the clouds to rapture his saints, so the slum worker

45. Roberts, *First Lessons on Money*.

46. For the practical impact of this theological shift on evangelical social reform movements, see Dayton, *Discovering an Evangelical Heritage*, 125–28.

established missions to rescue sinners out of the world to be among those who meet the Lord in the air. Evangelical effort that had once provided the impulse and troops for reform rallies was rechanneled into exegetical speculation about the timing of Christ's return.[47]

Free Methodists also gradually accepted premillennialism as it spread during the final three decades of the nineteenth century. For example, Wilson T. Hogue, a Free Methodist ordained by B. T. Roberts and later elected bishop, became an ardent supporter of premillennial eschatology. However, Roberts disagreed with Hogue and never adopted the premillennialism that would become so pervasive among his fellow evangelicals during his later years.[48]

Roberts articulated his own eschatological views in several articles published in the denominational periodicals *The Earnest Christian* and *The Free Methodist*. His foremost concern was to motivate Christians to live lives of holiness in the present day, regardless of which millennial view prevailed. Roberts commented on the scores of papers being published about eschatological theories in the 1880s:

> They are nothing but opinions, and prove nothing; therefore, of what use can they be? . . . Will the millennial theory as ventilated [in such articles] help us to comfort the sick and afflicted ones among us? Will the idea of a Christ coming one thousand years sooner, or later, assist us to lead souls to the Christ who came 1888 years ago?[49]

Thus, for Roberts, the issue was not about the timing of the millennium, but about present Christian faithfulness and holiness of life.

---

47. Ibid., 127. Dayton provides an interesting example resulting from this shift. Under the postmillennialism before the Civil War, Christians established liberal arts colleges that affirmed "the cultural values of this world," but the premillennialism of the post-Civil War era instead produced Bible schools to train evangelists for massive conversions.

48. Snyder, *Populist Saints*, 809.

49. Roberts, *Pungent Truths*, 106.

Yet Roberts' rejection of premillennialism is significant in understanding his choice to engage in Populist activism. Given the presuppositions of premillennial dispensationalism about the imminent return of Christ and the abandonment of this present world, many Christians abandoned social and political reform movements altogether, choosing instead to focus exclusively on the salvation of souls. If we know the boat is sinking, they reasoned, what good does it do to patch up the holes? Yet Roberts rejected such a denigration of the present world, choosing instead to invest in God's kingdom on earth through social reform.[50]

Roberts' alternative to the pessimism about human history so ubiquitous among premillennialists was to insist that humans do, in fact, have an active role to play in the unfolding of the kingdom of God on earth. Roberts never emphasized the role of human agency *to the exclusion of* divine action, as some later theologians of the Social Gospel Movement are accused of doing,[51] but he did insist that God utilizes human efforts to establish a provisional, limited peace prior to the *eschaton*. Like John Wesley, Roberts maintained an orthodox understanding of God's sovereign con-

---

50. Premillennialist dispensationalism still holds remarkable sway in American evangelicalism to this day, as evidenced by the millions of copies sold of *The Left Behind* series. N. T. Wright comments perceptively about the "just passing through" spirituality of premillennialism (which Roberts found troubling as well): "[It] encourages precisely a Gnostic attitude: the created world is at best irrelevant, at worst a dark, evil, gloomy place, and we immortal souls, who existed originally in a different sphere, are looking forward to returning to it as soon as we are allowed to" (Wright, *Surprised by Hope*, 90). For an examination of how premillennialism has also undermined environmental concern due to its devaluation of the earth, see Snyder, *Salvation Means Creation Healed*, 2–334, 55–62.

51. Walter Rauschenbusch, for example, suggests that the fate of humanity lies in human hands when he writes, "The great emancipation [of humanity] . . . will depend almost wholly on the moral forces which the Christian nations can bring to the fighting line against wrong" (Rauschenbusch, *Christianity and the Social*, 230). After reading such a statement, one wonders what role *God* plays in the grand project of human emancipation! It is my contention that B. T. Roberts, on the other hand, maintains a more sophisticated balance between the human and divine aspects of the kingdom of God than either premillennial dispensationalists or the proponents of the Social Gospel Movement.

trol over history while also preserving a robust theology of human freedom and agency. Roberts believed that humans could be properly called coworkers with God in the building of the kingdom. This conviction undergirded the entirety of his political activism. Snyder summarizes Roberts' views succinctly:

> Like Wesley, Roberts saw the church as God's instrument for justice and righteousness in society, not just for individual salvation. While Roberts insisted . . . that "Reform is not our salvation," he also insisted that the church, through revival and through Christians acting responsibly in society, was the key to social, political, and economic transformation.[52]

In summary, Roberts' Populist political thought and activism was grounded in his theological convictions about the centrality of God's concern for the poor, which emerged from his reading of Scripture, the transformative nature of salvation in both human hearts and in human society, and the role of human agency in the unfolding of the kingdom of God to be fully revealed at the *eschaton*. Together these rudimentary beliefs compelled Roberts to seek the spiritual, physical, economic, and political welfare of those to whom he ministered.

Roberts lived in challenging days. The desperation caused by economic depression, the marginalization of former ways of life by new technologies, the emergence for the first time of large monopolistic corporations—these all contributed to the woes of those to whom Roberts was ministering. Informed by his distinctively Wesleyan theological convictions, Roberts engaged in Populist activism because he felt that love compelled him to do so. Thus, Roberts built upon a theological foundation that was laid by his father in the faith, John Wesley, but he also expanded beyond what Wesley himself ever did in an effort to meet the unique challenges of his own day. In what follows, I hope to show how Roberts' populism represents the proper evolution and expansion of Wesleyan political theology.

---

52. Snyder, *Populist Saints*, 814.

3

Politics in the Wesleyan Spirit

As MENTIONED BRIEFLY IN chapter 1, Theodore Weber has argued quite convincingly that John Wesley remained a constitutional monarchist throughout his life. In support of this thesis, Weber demonstrates that during all three of the major political controversies that took place during his lifetime, John Wesley sided with the establishment, defending his king and country.[1] Weber concludes from his historical research into Wesley's involvement in these incidents that Wesley persistently "trumpeted the virtues of the existing system and projected disaster if it were destroyed and replaced; and he attacked the radical (liberal) ideology with its arguments for natural rights, popular sovereignty, and social contract. In these two fundamental respects he was obviously and undeniably a constitutional conservative."[2] Although Wesley did embrace some structural limits to the power of the monarchy—which is why he is rightly called a *constitutional* monarchist rather than an *absolute* monarchist—no amount of historical revisionism can

---

1. As mentioned previously on pages 7–8, the three controversies referred to here are the Jacobite Rebellion of 1745, the political agitation caused by John Wilkes and the Wilkites in the 1760s, and the American Colonial Rebellion of the late 1770s. See Weber, *Politics in the Order of Salvation*, 69–154.

2. Ibid., 110.

eliminate what Weber calls "the dominant problem" in Wesley's thinking: he consistently and univocally "defended a hierarchical, top-down concept of political authority and its consequent exclusion of the people from the political process."[3]

Here it is necessary to insert an important caveat. As surveyed in the first chapter, the hardline interpretation of Wesley as a staunch conservative is far from universally accepted. Certainly Wesley's activism in his later years—particularly his advocacy on behalf of the poor and his vocal opposition to the slave trade—ought, at the very least, to nuance any sweeping generalizations about Welsey's conservative Toryism. This is why Weber himself refers to Wesley as a "reconciled" Tory. Leon Hynson's discernment that Wesley supported the regulation of kingly authority, vocally championed human liberty, opposed the notion of the divine right of kings, and reserved a place for the liberty of an individual's conscience presents a necessary corrective to the "Wesley-as-monarchist" supposition.[4] It is unnecessary to re-present that debate here, since this has been fully discussed in the first chapter; however, modern readers of Wesley must always understand him, like all historical figures, in his own political and cultural context. To judge Wesley's political convictions in light of our own modern sensibilities will result in an unduly harsh interpretation. On the other hand, I agree with Weber's assessment of the basic problem for those of us who seek to make Wesley relevant for today's world: he simply did not insist strongly enough upon universal political agency. For those of us who believe that *all* people (gentry or commoner, landlord or tenant, black or white, female or male) ought to have a voice in the affairs of government, an effort must be made to reinterpret the undemocratic elements of Wesley's thought.[5]

3. Ibid., 391.

4. Hynson, "John Wesley's Concept," 38.

5. For Wesley, the primary aim in his debates with those favoring popular sovereignty was to preserve the biblical teaching found in Rom 13 that all authority comes down directly from God. In Wesley's mind, this necessarily excluded democratic commitments to popular sovereignty, since that would be an acknowledgment that political authority comes from below rather than from above. In 1772, Wesley wrote his "Thoughts Concerning the Origin of

In an effort to do just that, Weber proposes that Wesley's politics must be brought into conversation (and eventually submission) to his larger evangelical theology, specifically his articulation of the *ordo salutis* (or "order of salvation"). The problem with Wesley's political theology, according to Weber, is that Wesley does not integrate his political thinking into his soteriological thinking. Thus, in the final chapter of his book, Weber seeks to demonstrate

> how recovering the political image for Wesleyan theology draws politics into the order of salvation, thereby ending the exclusion of the people from the political process, and unifying the God of politics and the God of the *ordo salutis* as the Holy Trinity whose governing of a fallen world provides context and guidance for the political vocation of mankind. Also, it will serve the broader purposes of Wesleyan theological development by requiring attention to the *whole* image of God in place of the exclusive attention usually given to the moral image.[6]

In his sermon "The New Birth," John Wesley identifies three specific ways in which God created humanity in his own image. He terms these the "natural" image, the "political" image, and the "moral" image. For Wesley, humanity's ability to think, reason, and act freely constitutes what it means to be made in the *natural* image of God. With this comes the capability of mankind to know God and obey his laws. The *political* image refers to humankind's unique role as stewards over creation, having been given dominion over all of the creatures of the earth according to God's will. Such a stewardship ought to be characterized by charity and benevolence, reflecting the long-suffering patience of God. And finally, the *moral* image of mankind refers to the fullness of love, which governs "all of [her or] his tempers, thoughts, words, and actions." Women

---

Power" in which he attacks the notion that the people ought to be governed by their own consent and instead reasserts "the sovereignty of God over the political process" (Weber, *Politics in the Order of Salvation*, 104). As tensions rise with the colonies in America, Wesley writes this piece to persuade his readers, "'The supposition, then, that the people are the origin of power, is every way indefensible" (*Works [Jackson]*, 11:53, §21).

6. Weber, *Politics in the Order of Salvation*, 392.

and men, in their original, unfallen state, reflected the love, justice, mercy, truth, and purity of God himself.[7]

Each of these three aspects of the divine image has been negatively impacted by the fall. The moral image of mankind was utterly lost and destroyed in the fall such that humanity is now naturally prone toward idolatry, selfishness, and sinfulness. And although some aspects of the natural image remain, its primary functions—namely knowledge of, love for, and obedience to God—have been lost. Humans became incapable of perceiving the presence of God and thus have "lost their freedom to know, to obey, and to love God."[8] This freedom is only partially awakened within man through the work of God's prevenient grace.

Similarly, the political image of God has also been damaged. The original design of responsible stewardship and care by humanity over creation degenerated, as a result of the fall, into a relationship of exploitation and hostility. As a result of the spiritual depravity of humankind, creation no longer receives blessing from human governance, but instead suffers under human exploitation. Mankind remains in the dominant position, but does not properly steward this responsibility. Weber summarizes the result of the fall on the political image thus: "The *constitution* of the political image has not been lost, but the *representational aspect* of imaging has been redirected."[9] Humankind now lords over creation through self-interest rather than through benevolent care, as God's will demands.

Despite articulating these three distinct aspects of what it means to be made in the image of God in his sermon "The New Birth," Wesley spends very little time discussing the implications of the *political* image. He elaborates on the *moral* image the most, writing and preaching at great length about the need for God to restore humanity into a place of holiness, sanctification, and perfect love. Weber finds this a lamentable shortcoming in Wesley's theology, since affirming the restoration of the *moral* image of

---

7. Wesley, "Sermon 45: The New Birth," In *Works*, 2:193, §I.1.

8. Vickers, "Wesley's Theological Emphases," 195.

9. Weber, *Politics in the Order of Salvation*, 395.

God necessarily has profound implications on the *political* image as well. Weber writes,

> [Wesley's] preoccupation is almost exclusively with the *moral* image. Apparently he found neither the natural nor the political images very interesting, except through extension of concern for the moral image, for he made no sustained effort to explore their meaning and implications and make them into important elements of his theology.[10]

This prevented Wesley from developing a properly Methodist political theology, a task that is now left to those who are heirs of the Wesleyan tradition.

So this is the agenda of Weber's final chapter: to extend the theological presuppositions of Wesley's soteriology into the political realm. In short, he attempts to offer a fully developed theology of the *political image*, since Wesley himself left this project unfinished. Weber suggests that a modern Wesleyan political theology will be composed of five crucial characteristics.

THE CHARACTERISTICS OF A WESLEYAN POLITICAL THEOLOGY

First, Weber insists that any properly Christian political theology will reflect our basic convictions about God's Trinitarian nature. Fundamentally, Christians believe that God is *tres Personae, una Substantia*. At the heart of God's Trinitarian nature is mutuality and communal concern. There has externally existed a reciprocal dynamism at the heart of the relationship between the three Persons of the Trinity—an aspect of God's ontological being often described as *perichoretic* or interpenetrating.[11] This depiction of

10. Ibid., 410. Italics in the original.

11. Elaborating at length upon this essential aspect of God's nature would go far beyond the scope of this book, but the centrality of the Trinitarian nature of God to all of Christian theology is undergoing something of a renaissance recently due to the work of theologians such as Wolfhart Pannenberg, Jürgen Moltmann, John Zizioulas, and Miroslav Volf, to name just a few. For

the Godhead stands in sharp contract to unorthodox Monarchianism, which upholds political models of strong, centralized, unified power concentrated within a single individual, such as that found in monarchies and dictatorships. Moltmann eloquently articulates the dangers inherent in focusing on the *oneness* of God to the exclusion of his *threeness*:

> As long as the unity of the triune God is understood monadically or subjectivistically, and not in Trinitarian terms, the whole cohesion of a religious legitimation of [tyrannical] political sovereignty continues to exist. It is only when the doctrine of the Trinity vanquishes the monotheistic notion of the great universal monarch in heaven, and his divine patriarchs in the world, that earthly rulers, dictators and tyrants cease to find any justifying religious archetypes anymore.[12]

Weber, in agreement with Moltmann, argues not only that the best forms of human government must imitate the mutuality and consociational structure embedded within God's being, but that the Trinity must also provide the theological foundation for government's agenda (i.e., redeeming, ordering, preserving, and developing human flourishing).[13] The contrast between the monarchical view and Trinitarian view as it pertains to political theology can be illustrated in this way:

---

an excellent exposition on how the Trinitarian nature of God ought to impact political theology, see especially Jürgen Moltmann's *Trinity and the Kingdom of God*, 129–32, 151–78, 191–222. Moltmann argues persuasively that whereas Arianism and Sabellianism misunderstand the relationship of Christ to the Father and thereby undermine the Trinitarian formulation of the Godhead (consequently upholding political monarchies), a properly orthodox perspective on the *perichoretic* activity of the communion of God as Three-in-One provides a theological rationale for mutuality, community, and decentralized authority in political structures.

12. Moltmann, *Trinity and the Kingdom of God*, 197.

13. Weber, *Politics in the Order of Salvation*, 395–96; Moltmann, *Trinity and the Kingdom of God*, 191–222.

Monarchical	Trinitarian
• imperial • distant from mankind • top-down and hierarchical • distinct possibility of tyrrany • ruling	• reciprocal • incarnational and relational • reciprocity and community • power limited by checks and balances • redeeming

Because human governance must serve as a reflection of the governance of God over all of creation—governance committed to redemption and reconciliation—politics is properly understood as an essential part of the order of salvation. Weber points out that this stands in contrast to the political theology of Martin Luther, who denied that the gospel message had direct implications on the political order. Contrary to this sharp division between politics on the one hand and the gospel on the other, Weber insists that Wesleyan theology integrates the two, since government (properly understood) is a legitimate means by which humans fulfill their God-given mission of stewarding all of creation and caring benevolently for both human and non-human creation as a reflection of divine love.[14] In short, the starting point of all Wesleyan political

14. Here Weber argues that governing principles must be rooted not in Thomistic natural law, but solely in the principles of divine revelation, since "human nature as such tells us nothing of the meaning and work of government" (ibid., 397). At this point, however, I believe Weber underestimates the extent to which human moral capacities have been restored through the work of God's prevenient grace. If indeed God's prevenient grace is at work in all of creation, convicting men of sin and drawing them to God, then I believe we may approach natural law (albeit cautiously) as a proper source for understanding the justice and righteousness of God. Indeed, I believe a robust appreciation of Wesley's doctrine of prevenient grace (which Wesley understood soteriologically, but which in my view can also be applied politically) lends itself to a greater appreciation for the fruitfulness of political principles derived from anthropology. By overlooking the universal work of prevenient grace in all of humankind, I believe Weber offers an unfairly negative assessment of human nature at this juncture.

theology is "the doctrine of God in this Trinitarian sense."[15] Because human beings are made in the political image of God, they share in the Trinity's mission of redemption. Politics is thus participation in the order of salvation as it is revealed in God's triune nature.

Second, Weber believes that because *all* humans have been created in God's political image, any proper political process will be inclusive of *all* people. On this particular point we encounter great tension (perhaps even contradiction) with the Tory political convictions of John Wesley himself. To be fair, Wesley was simply affirming the precepts of the English constitution of his day. Yet he never critiqued the limitations placed by that constitution on what type of person was allowed to have political agency. To the chagrin of many of his theological heirs, Wesley unswervingly maintained:

> that political responsibility belonged only to those who held political office. The rest of the people should obey those in authority over them, and go about their proper business, but not presume to involve themselves in matters of governance and public policy.[16]

Wesley was convinced that the precepts established by the English constitution were consistent with Scripture, despite its exclusion of large sections of the populace from having a political voice.[17] Furthermore, he questioned the competence of the average person to make political judgments.[18] In this sense, Wesley was

---

15. Ibid., 397.

16. Ibid., 399. Interestingly, Wesley himself didn't exactly remain faithful to this conviction, as we have noted already in his opposition to slavery and vocal advocacy for economic reform.

17. Again, this is likely only the result of his historical location. There seems to be no indication that Wesley examined the English constitution critically in light of biblical principles of universality and inclusiveness. But this is why Weber (and I) insist that Wesley's political views ought to be submitted to the insights of his soteriological views, which were far more universal in scope.

18. Wesley once wrote a hypothetical speech for William Pitt in which he has Pitt declare, "How came these colliers and keelman to be so well acquainted with affairs of State? . . . Do they comprehend the balance of Europe? Do they know the weakness and strength of its several kingdoms; the characters of

the polar opposite of a Populist (since the very term "populism" is derived from the word for "the people") and he made no apologies for his stance.

However, Wesley's exclusion of the people from the political process is in direct contradiction to key aspects of his theology as well as with his habit of entrusting common men and women with leadership roles in the Methodist movement.[19] Since, as we have said, all of humankind has been made in God's image, and since one important aspect of that image is the *political* image, it becomes theologically untenable to maintain that vast numbers of these humans ought to be excluded from the political process. God intended all people to reflect his image through their responsible, caring stewardship over creation. This is a responsibility given to humans by God, and it is indeed part of what makes us human. We are, all of us, "political by divine creation."[20] This does not necessarily imply that direct democracy is the only legitimate form of government. Representative political institutions are necessary for the governance of large modern nations, and these institutions are instituted by the best of human reason (a reflection of the *natural* image) for the purpose of fulfilling the vocation of the *political* image.[21] However, any distinction between a political class and nonpolitical class (as once existed between whites and blacks, property holders and the landless, and men and women) must be

---

the Monarchs and their Ministers; the springs of this and that public motion? . . . 'Let them mind their own work,' keep to their pits and keels, and leave State affairs to me" (Wesley, "Thoughts on the Present State of Public Affairs in a Letter to a Friend (1766)," in *Works* (Jackson), 11:19). It is hard to image more undemocratic political rhetoric!

19. The contrast here is made all the more remarkable when we consider the extent to which Wesley empowered women and lay people to minister within the classes, bands, and societies of the early Methodist movement. Wesley entrusted the common people to take leadership roles during the revival and to spread the gospel, yet apparently did not trust these same people to elect national representatives to Parliament! Why did Wesley never recognize such obvious tensions—if not, outright contradictions—in his own views?

20. Weber, *Politics in the Order of Salvation*, 399.

21. Ibid., 400.

condemned as contradictory to the biblical teaching that all humans have been made in God's image.

Third, Weber asserts that the authorization of political power must come from God *through the people*. Once again, Wesley denied this. In his view, all governing authority is granted from above without the people's consent. Wesley believed that the teaching of Scripture plainly stated that rulers govern at the behest of God alone. Unsurprisingly, these views surfaced frequently in Wesley's writing during the American colonial rebellion. In his statement "A Calm Address to Our American Colonies," Wesley stated, "In wide-extended dominions, a very small part of the people are concerned in making laws. This, as all public business, must be done by delegation, the delegates are chosen by a select number. And those that are not electors, who are far the greater part, *stand by, idle and helpless spectators.*"[22] In Wesley's mind, then, the people had no role in legitimating their government (hence his opposition to American independence); rather, God alone legitimates all governmental authority.

Here again Wesley is exposed to critique for betraying his own theological convictions. For Weber sees in the doctrine of the political image—an image stamped upon *all* people—an argument "that anyone exercising authority in political society through political office does so by some receiving of authority from the people, who corporately under God are given the task of governance. No one can govern authoritatively apart from this process of consent."[23] Thus, God still grants authority, but he does so indirectly. God has granted authority to the people who then, in turn, pass along and delegate that authority to particular offices and elected individuals. The difference in these views can be illustrated thus:

---

22. Wesley, "A Calm Address to Our American Colonies (1775)," in *Works (Jackson)*, 11:80–86, emphasis mine.

23. Weber, *Politics in the Order of Salvation*, 401.

Wesley's View of Authority   **Weber's View of Authority**

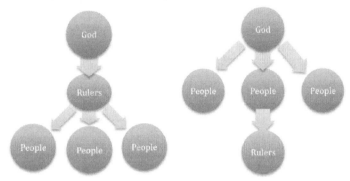

Fourth, Weber maintains that a consistently Wesleyan political theology will encourage and uphold principles of self-government. The political image of God not only gives humankind the right to rule over the animals, but also over themselves. This is a question of political agency: the freedom to act politically, effect policies, and even overturn government should it because oppressive. For although the political image of man was marred by the fall, it was not utterly destroyed. Certainly, man's ability to govern over himself has led to brutal dictatorships and unjust regimes. However, humankind has not lost the ability to authorize power and exercise its use. Taken together with his previous point, we can summarize Webber's view this way: government ought to be *by* the people and *for* the people. The people provide both political authorization and political agency in any properly Wesleyan political theology.

Fifth and finally, Weber articulates the desired nature of political institutions—what he terms "societal instruments of the purposes of God"[24]—given the principle of the political image. He argues that since governments must fundamentally be concerned with the flourishing of both human and non-human creation, the use of power ought to be directed toward the following ends: 1) environmental protection and development, 2) promoting the common good through such means as public education, providing

24. Ibid., 405.

basic resources for the poor, promoting private and public health, or fostering the arts, and 3) equipping and enabling all human beings to be able to "fulfill their political vocation of imaging God."[25] Thus, the primary evaluative questions that Christians must ask about any form of political power is:

> How [does it] fit into and serve the whole-making work of God, expressed in the Old Testament as *shalom* and in the New Testament as reconciliation? [Does it] help bring about God's creation to the fullness of its possibilities? In a world deranged by sin, [does it] provide defense against further damage and disruption . . . and encourage and facilitate the overcoming of brokenness (the work of redemption and renewal)?[26]

If the principles of Wesley's doctrine of the political image are followed to their logical conclusion, Weber argues, then any proper and legitimate form of government will embody these five characteristics. To summarize, government must be 1) reciprocal rather than hierarchical, 2) inclusive of *all* people, 3) aware that political authority comes *through* the people, 4) protective of the freedom of self-government and agency of the people, and 5) composed of political institutions directed toward creational and human flourishing. This does not necessarily mandate that governments must be democracies; it merely requires as theologically necessary that all governments direct their "processes, institutions

---

25. Ibid., 406. It must be noted that the vision Weber offers here of a society that enables human flourishing and that lives in harmony with creation bears a striking resemblance to Wesley's own vision of holistic salvation. Especially during the final two decades of his life, Wesley believed that a coming "Great Revival" would sweep across the globe, transforming human hearts and human societies by the power of the Holy Spirit. For more on the mature Wesley's eschatology and how it impacted his socioeconomic views, see Maddox, "Nurturing the New Creation," 21–52. Although Wesley did not envision this taking place primarily through governmental structures, the *telos* of both Weber's political vision and Wesley's theological vision bear striking resemblance. As Maddox has suggested, this indicates that Wesley (perhaps unconsciously) set a healthy trajectory toward a holistic view of salvation (and politics!) that can be embraced by modern scholars.

26. Ibid., 407–408.

and personnel toward the care of the creation and the nurturing and enablement of members of the community in the fulfilling of their political vocation."[27]

B. T. ROBERTS: FULFILLING THE WEBER THESIS

Given such criteria, the nineteenth-century American Populist B. T. Roberts embodied a more thoroughly and consistently Wesleyan political theology than John Wesley himself. If we accept Weber's insight that the development of Wesley's doctrine of the political image necessitates greater human freedom and popular political agency, then we find in Roberts a fulfillment of a robust Wesleyan political praxis. He does so in three key ways.

First, B. T. Robert's political theology presents a more rigorous commitment to the universal political agency of all people than does John Wesley's political theology. Theologically, the commitment to the universality of the political image is analogous to Wesley's belief that God intends to restore the image of God in all people through his prevenient, justifying, and sanctifying grace. Wesley applied this limitless optimism of God's grace soteriologically, but not politically, as mentioned previously. Roberts, by contrast, finds no problem in transferring these soteriological commitments into the political realm. Hence, Roberts travels about spreading tracts, speaking at conventions, and organizing at the grassroots because he fundamentally believes in empowering the people to act for themselves. Because the people to whom Roberts ministers are created in the *imago Dei*, he commits himself to actualizing their political agency in a society that is systematically excluding them from the democratic process and robbing them of their economic welfare.

Roberts' commitment to Populist politics grew out of both his Wesleyan theology and his American cultural ethos, as it did for many clergy and laymen in nineteenth-century America. Timothy L. Smith, in his now classic work *Revivalism and Social Reform*,

27. Ibid., 409.

points out that Wesleyan-Arminian theology spread rapidly during the fervent revivals of mid-nineteenth-century America. Soteriologically, the traditional Calvinist emphasis on election was gradually replaced by the Arminian insistence upon the availability of the gospel to *all* people who freely choose to respond in faith, with the result that "the roaring revivals of the 1850s . . . broke the grip of Calvinism on nineteenth century Protestantism."[28] The pervasive themes of Wesleyan-Arminianism—such as unlimited atonement and individual freedom—were better suited to the democratic and egalitarian ethos of American politics.[29]

But the reasons behind Roberts' populism are not exclusively theological. He was certainly impacted, as are all theologians, by the cultural milieu in which he lived. From its very beginning, America has always valued egalitarianism over hierarchy. Sociologists of religion may debate whether America's democratic politics were fueled by theology or whether theology was fueled by politics, but most likely the answer is found somewhere in the middle, and each proved formative in Roberts' thinking.[30] Given

28. Smith, *Revivalism and Social Reform*, 102.

29. For another noteworthy resource that places Roberts in context, see Hatch, *Democratization of American*. See especially ibid., 83–91 for a description of how the Methodism of Roberts' youth had come to embrace Populist forms of spirituality and praxis. Hatch notes three primary ways that the church incarnated itself into American Populist culture: first, by denying the traditional distinction between clergy and laity; second, by elevating individual spiritual experience above traditional doctrines and learned orthodoxy; and third, by believing that this lay-centered church could usher in a new era of freedom by overthrowing authoritarian structures and replacing such structures with self-agency (ibid., 9–11). The parallels between this wider religious ethos and the Populist nature of Roberts' politics are readily apparent.

30. Mark A. Noll notes the ways that more Arminian, evangelical forms of faith were better suited to the American context even dating back to pre-revolutionary times: "The types of religion active in Pre-Revolutionary America were variously disposed toward a democratic revolution . . . And evangelicalism inspired by face-to-face itinerant preaching, that stressed the all-powerful but also egalitarian grace of God as the source of salvation, that taught converts to connect virtue to the exertions of their hearts instead of to mere social conformity—this was a religion already closer to democracy than the hierarchical establishmentarian communalism of either clerically ordered Congregationalism or inherited Anglicanism" (Noll, *America's God*, 192).

the radically different cultural context in America than in Wesley's England, it is no surprise, then, that Roberts embraced democratic and egalitarian forms of politics, but this does not diminish the thesis that his political views were more consistent with Wesleyan theology than Wesley's Toryism.

Any yet Roberts was more than just a promoter of democracy; he was a Populist. It is not by mistake that Howard Snyder entitled his biography of B. T. and Ellen Roberts *Populist Saints*. Populism, as we have already mentioned in chapter 2, can be understood as an *extreme* form of democracy. As Snyder explains, "The essence of Populism is that the people (*all* the people, fairly represented, and especially the common people and oppressed) should control the government and that the test of the faithful, legitimate government is the people's general welfare."[31] He continues: "This is nothing more than the ideal enshrined in America's founding documents. By the 1870s and 1880s, however, it sounded radical and even subversive."[32] Concerns for the *people*—that they be properly represented, that their rights be defended, and that their ability of be self-governing remain uninhibited—are the hallmark of Roberts' politics. In this sense, Roberts fulfills what Weber longs to see: a Wesleyan theology robustly committed to defending the political image of God found in all people.

In sharp contrast to this populism, we find that John Wesley maintained a deep suspicion of democratic political movements. This suspicion surfaced quite conspicuously during the Wilkite upheaval of the 1760s. Wesley opposed the libertine John Wilkes on the grounds that his advocacy for greater liberty and increased voting rights could spread disorder until "the people will be inflamed more and more; the torrent will swell higher and higher, till at length it bursts through all opposition, and overflows the land . . . [which will] become a field of blood."[33] Wesley feared democracy as destabilizing and referred to those who promoted it as

---

31. Snyder, *Populist Saints*, 787.

32. Ibid., 787.

33. John Wesley, "Thoughts on Liberty," February 24, 1772, in *Works (Jackson)*, 11:28.

"King Mob."[34] Wesley believed, as did the other conservatives of his day, that only property-owning males ought to have the right to vote and staunchly defended the precepts of the constitution of 1689 against those who wished to democratize the British system. Weber succinctly states Wesley's position: "However greatly Mr. Wesley may have loved the common people, he clearly did not respect their aptitude for political commentary, and he certainly did not want to entrust to them a role in political decision making."[35] This illustrates one important instance of how Roberts' politics are more firmly committed to the universal political image of God—and the practical implications of this doctrine—than was Wesley.

Second, Roberts critiques hierarchies of political and economic power. If, as Weber contends, "the tendency in governing introduced with the concept of political imaging is toward the creating and eliciting of counterforces, the initial formation of a consciousness of rights, and the attempt to begin the subordination of power to law,"[36] then B. T. Roberts manifests a prime example of political imaging actualized in his nineteenth-century American context. Central to Roberts' political convictions and actions is a deep and abiding concern for the marginalized, accompanied by attempts to organize such people for the purpose of challenging the hegemony of concentrated economic power.

Roberts blamed the plight of his fellow farmers not on their substandard work ethic or the poor quality of their crops, but rather on those possessing economic power who abused their position in order to gain riches for themselves at the expense of the poor farmer. For example, in January of 1889, Roberts published an article in the denominational paper *The Free Methodist* in which he denounced those economic "measures which have a direct tendency to impoverish the many in order to enrich the few."[37] At issue is the prevailing hierarchy of political and economic power,

34. Ibid., 11:28.

35. Weber, *Politics in the Order of Salvation*, 98.

36. Ibid., 408–409.

37. Roberts, quoted in Snyder, "How B. T. Roberts Voted."

which enables the rich to grow richer while the poor become even poorer. In the same editorial he went on to claim,

> The cause of the growing poverty of farmers is not natural but artificial. It is found in the combinations made by those engaged in other productive industries, and in transportation, by means of which the proper proportion is destroyed between the prices of what the farmer has to sell and what he wishes to buy. Because of these combinations, and the laws which render them possible, the farmer is compelled to give two days' work of his own, for one day's work of the man who made any article which he buys.[38]

Roberts responded to this crisis, as we have already recounted, by organizing and promoting the Farmers' Alliance in his native New York state. Indeed, both the Farmers' Alliance and the larger Populist movement that emerged from it can be described as "counterforces" (to use Weber's word) working against those legal and systematic structures that effectively marginalized an entire class of people.

Third, Roberts embodies Weber's conviction that government ought to work to promote the common good and the general welfare of all people. Whereas Wesley did, on rare occasions, acknowledge the role that government had to play in ensuring the general welfare (such concerns are particularly intimated at in his "Thoughts on the Present Scarcity of Provisions"), the locus of Wesley's politics remained at the level of the individual. Societal transformation, for Wesley, was the natural culmination of transformed individual hearts. Compared to later Methodists, there is relatively little awareness in Wesley of the nature of systemic and structural causes to social ills—a fact that is, again, most likely merely the result of his historical and geographic location.[39]

38. Roberts, quoted in Snyder, *Populist Saints*, 785.

39. Randy Maddox argues, however, that Wesley did exhibit a certain amount of social concern in his later years as he became increasingly committed to a postmillennial eschatology. See especially Maddox, "Nurturing the New Creation," 40–51. Nevertheless, the extent of Wesley's awareness of the ability to harness political institutions for addressing structural issues was not

But Roberts, on the other hand, held to a positive view of the government's ability to promote the common good. Rooted in the optimism so characteristic of the nineteenth-century American revivalists, Roberts exhorted his people to become involved in politics, insisting that to do so was a proper expression of Christian discipleship. Roberts did not think twice about joining hands with non-Christians in the secular realm in order to achieve the proper aim of politics: enacting and legislating justice on behalf of the marginalized.[40] Indeed, the guiding biblical principle of *dikaiosune*, which is Greek for "justice" or "righteousness," undergirded all of his political efforts, whether they were on behalf of slaves, women, or the poor. Howard Snyder comments on the relevance of Roberts' politics for our own day:

> In working to establish the Farmers' Alliance, Roberts was addressing a vital issue that continues to be of great relevance. How can power—particularly economic and political power—be harnessed and channeled for the public good—for the benefit of all, especially those with little or no power? How can the people control their political and economic institutions so they can exist for the public good and are not exploitative or co-opted for the benefit of special interests?[41]

These crucial concerns are precisely what Weber contends must constitute a genuinely Wesleyan political theology—and we find them at every turn, animating and enlivening Roberts' political action.

In summary, B. T. Roberts offers an example of what Wesleyan politics, rooted in the doctrine of the political image of God, will look like in action. Taken together, the picture that emerges of Roberts' political theology is far more consistent with Weber's

---

as extensive as Roberts.' Of course, Roberts had the benefit of another century of human history, a century of increasing recognition within Europe and North America that political institutions can be utilized for the benefit of all people.

40. Snyder, *Populist Saints*, 787.

41. Ibid., 788.

vision of humankind bearing the political image of God than was Wesley's own politics. Furthermore, Roberts' democratic populism resonates with the Trinitarian (as opposed to monarchical) forms of government mentioned earlier. Whereas Wesley clung to his monarchical models of government, we find in Roberts a politics that empowers humankind, generates reciprocity between those who govern and the governed, and catalyzes community. These are precisely the characteristics that must constitute a genuinely Wesleyan political theology.[42]

In the final chapter of his book, Weber offers a compelling vision of what happens when the prevenient grace of God works in political systems to renew creation:

> We may take as evidences of prevenient grace those oc-casions when emerging public consciousness discerns the purpose of government to be *service to the members of the political community and not to their rulers; when it discovers the notion of individual and group rights and perceives the need for protecting them with customs, laws, and structures of power;* when it recognizes the necessity to draw the people into the political process—initially to serve their self-interest and draw upon their wisdom, but ultimately to create the possibility for them to fulfill their political vocation under God.[43]

Weber offers a compelling vision indeed—a vision I believe is embodied remarkably well in the life and work of the little-known Methodist farmer and Populist B. T. Roberts.

---

42. Weber, *Politics in the Order of Salvation*, 411.

43. Ibid., 412. Emphasis added.

Conclusion

As I write the conclusion of this book, our nation and world has just endured what can only be described as a truly horrific summer. War broke out once again between Israel and the Palestinians. Tensions continue to mount with Russia over Ukraine and their invasion of Crimea earlier in the year. Police dressed in military gear continue to clash with protesters in Ferguson, Missouri, following the shooting death of Michael Brown. ISIS poses an increasing threat in Syria and Iraq as we hear accounts of horrendous acts of persecution against Christians and Yazidis in those areas. In the midst of such events, Christians must be asking themselves, "What does it mean to live faithfully in such a world?"

Unfortunately for the witness and mission of the church, Christians today are not united on how to engage in the political issues of our day. The church is divided between the right and the left just as much as society at large, with those on the right claiming that the left has abandoned the basics of the faith while the left screams at the right for being closed-minded and backwards.

I do not pretend to be able, in this small volume, to bridge that wide chasm that has formed over the decades of the so-called "culture wars." Nor do I offer a magical remedy to the bitter partisanship that seems to have a chokehold on American politics and, all too often, on the American church as well. However, in this conclusion, I would like to offer some very practical observations that have emerged from this study of two Christian men who, in their own ways, genuinely sought after an authentic form of public

Christian faith. Undoubtedly, even these very basic suggestions may prove divisive to some, yet they are offered in the hope that, as followers of Jesus, we who seek the flourishing of humankind may keep first things first.

1. Wesleyan Politics insists that the public sphere, too, is under the Lordship of Christ.

This may at first seem to be quite an obvious observation. However, if one truly comes to believe it, as I think John Wesley began to see late in his life and as B. T. Roberts saw as well, then this conviction will radically altar how one behaves "out there." For quite a long time, many Christians have been guided by an unwritten assumption—which is utterly foreign to the world of the Hebrew Scriptures and the New Testament—that faith is a matter pertaining to one's private, inner, "spiritual" life and that it excludes that sphere of the outward, physical, and social world. As a result, many well-meaning Christians tend to hyper-spiritualize the message of Jesus. Yet Jesus bumped up against the political authorities, challenging them to such an extent that they killed him. And when Christ defined his own mission[1] he was making a political statement. If, then, Jesus came proclaiming a new kingdom that operated by a different set of rules—an upside-down kingdom that lifted up the poor, the prisoners, the handicapped, and the oppressed—then what makes us who claim to follow him think that we can live differently than him? If we are *not* getting into trouble for our political solidarity with the marginalized, then something is terribly wrong: we have hyper-spiritualized the message of Jesus.

---

1. "The Spirit of the Lord is on me because he has anointed me to preach good news to the poor. He has sent me to proclaim freedom for the prisoners and recovery of sight to the blind, to set the oppressed free, and to proclaim the Year of Jubilee" (Luke 4:18–19).

2. Wesleyan politics focuses primarily on people, not issues.

The Free Methodist Society of Saint Charles, Illinois, in 1878,
courtesy of the Marston Memorial Historical Archives.

A striking similarity between both John Wesley and B. T. Roberts
is that both men were driven to political advocacy and action as
a direct result of their pastoral work. When Wesley witnessed
the abject poverty of the people to whom he preached and with
whom he prayed, he was forced to ask why. This led him to voice
his concerns about some of the economic structures that contributed to hunger. Roberts, in the same way, witnessed firsthand the
dire need of the farmers in New York, and this motivated him
to organize politically. Contrast this with how Christians often
approach politics today: We form an "opinion" about an "issue"
based upon something we have read on Facebook or seen on TV.
Little personal interaction is involved. Yet a Wesleyan approach to
politics is rooted in the primary truth that all people are created in
the image of God and that all of creation is intended to reflect the
community of the holy Triune God, with whom we will one day be

united after having been sanctified through the power of the Spirit. This means that first and foremost our political theology must be people-centric, not issue-centric. For the Christian, immigration is not an *issue*; it is about *people* for whom Christ died. For the Christian, poverty is not an *issue*; it is about *people* made in God's image. For the Christian, the choice to go to war is not an *issue* to be theoretically debated, but about people that God is wooing to himself through his prevenient grace.

Closely related to this, I would add that Christian politics is a local politics. It grows organically from one's own particular context, location, and relationships. While I was a pastor in an economically underdeveloped area of Indianapolis, I originally focused nearly all of my attention on my church and their "spiritual" needs. However, it soon became apparent to me that many of them were suffering for both spiritual and physical reasons. So I continued to care for them on a spiritual level, but to also speak out against the predatory lenders in our neighborhood who, by charging unfairly high interest rates, had practically made some of my congregants into indentured servants. I wrote a letter to the *Indianapolis Star* about how the lottery preys upon the poor more than any other demographic (for which I received a lot of hate mail: "Stick with the gospel, preacher"). And when the city threatened to close our local library branch as well as five other branches located in impoverished neighborhoods, I mobilized our neighbors and called on the media to pressure the mayor, who was up for re-election. Eventually, our efforts were successful, and Mayor Ballard pledged to keep all the libraries open. The catalyst for all such actions, though, was always personal relationships. Why did I want to save the library? Because a teenager in my church asked me, "Pastor, where will I go in the winter when it gets cold outside and my dad comes home drunk and he wants to hit me?" Relationships motivate Christian political action.

3. Compelled by love, Wesleyan politics seeks the common good.

By suggesting that we seek the common good, I do not mean that we embrace some idealistic do-gooderism that ignores the gravity of human evil in the world. As Saint Augustine has taught us, any peace in this era (*saeculum*) will necessarily be an incomplete, temporary, and provisional peace. Rather, I mean to suggest that by recapturing a robust doctrine of the power of the Holy Spirit to work within the human heart, transforming and sanctifying us to make us like Christ and thereby enabling us to experience ever widening circles of love for the human—and nonhuman—creatures around us, we can devote ourselves fully to the work of the flourishing of creation.

Much Christian preaching today, particularly in conservative evangelical circles, reflects an especially strong pessimism about the future of the social order. Sermons about the decay of the moral fabric of society, lamentations of the decline of traditional values, and so forth seem ubiquitous in certain slices of America. Such attitudes generally emerge from, I would argue, a premillennial dispensationalist eschatology that is decidedly inconsistent with the thought of either John Wesley or B. T. Roberts. In fact, both men were convinced that, on the contrary, the Spirit of God was doing a mighty work in the world, transforming human hearts and even whole societies. Not only this, but humanity could mysteriously participate in this work alongside with God, somehow contributing to the grand project of the kingdom. This kingdom, which has been inaugurated but has not yet been fully realized, beckons us all to a life of purpose beyond mere self-interest and acquisition, but instead to a life to self-giving, sacrificial, radical peacemaking and demonstrating a way of life that foreshadows the Reality that is to come.

American individualism has, without a doubt, produced an incredibly efficient system for generating wealth. It has spurred innovation and hard work. Yet in the process, many American Christians have been more Americanized than Christianized, allowing their value for individualism to veil the biblical injunction to bear one another's burdens and to seek the common good. Roberts offers an example that counters this. He witnessed a state of affairs in which the urban elite continued to make the rules and acquire more and more wealth while the rural farmers struggled to even eat. Compelled by the love of a pastor's heart, Roberts took action on their behalf.

4. Wesleyan politics has always had a "preferential option for the poor."

The witness of Wesley and Roberts regarding the poor is univocal and unequivocal: they hold a special place in God's heart and therefore Christians must show them special care. As this book has demonstrated, a Wesleyan response to poverty must be holistic— concerned with body, soul, and mind. When in 1747 and 1748 Wesley saw that some of the poor of London were without medicine, he took special collections, personally begging people for money in order to create medicine dispensaries, and Wesley himself even treated some of the impoverished patients who were afflicted with the most basic illnesses.[2] He instructed his fellow Methodists to not merely give to the poor, but to form relationships with them. For Wesley, it was fundamentally about "bridging the gulf between the strata of society."[3] His word to the Methodist stewards: "Put yourself in the place of every poor man, and deal with him just as you would God would deal with you."[4] And to a wealthy, educated member of the upper class named Miss March, Wesley pleaded that she leave her social circle to be with the poor, writing,

> Go and see the poor and sick in their own poor little hovels. Take up your cross, woman! Remember the faith! Jesus went before you, and will go with you. Put off the

---

2. Wesley, *Letters*, 2:307.

3. Marquardt, *John Wesley's Social Ethics*, 30.

4. Quoted in ibid., 34.

gentlewoman; you bear an [*sic.*] higher character. You are
an heir of God and joint-heir with Christ![5]

What might it look like if the so-called "respectable" church
of today addressed the politics of poverty with similar zeal and
sacrifice? Imagine if the American church's response to the recent
healthcare crisis had been similar to Wesley's reaction in London.
What if the church and families within the church, instead of only
sending checks to charities, began to reverse the trend of "white
flight" that took place in the 1950s and 60s and actually started
moving back into urban neighborhoods in order to live as an in-
carnational presence among the economically disadvantaged? Or,
taking Roberts as our example, what if the church actually stood
in solidarity with those who protest unfair labor laws designed to
benefit large corporations at the expense of individual workers? I
suggest that engaging in such political practices would not only
witness to the world of Christ's love and further the spread of the
good news of the gospel, but it would also spiritually revive the
Christians themselves who engage in such acts of mercy. One of
Wesley's keenest insights into the nature of human spirituality was
this: caring for the least of these is a means of grace not only for the
one who receives the care, but even more for the one who gives it.
Yet he had discovered nothing new. Christ himself taught that "it
is more blessed to give than to receive" (Acts 20:35).

5. Wesleyan Politics lives between Rom 13 and Rev 13.

The tension that both Wesley and Roberts lived within—the tension that all Christians have been living in since the Pentecost—
can be described as that space between Rom 13 and Rev 13. Of
course, Rom 13 is a well-known passage in which Paul appeals to
Christians to submit to the governing authorities since no authority on earth exists except those that have been established by God
(v. 1). This text is frequently cited in debates concerning submission to authorities, Christians in the military, civil disobedience,

---

5. Wesley, "Letter to Miss March," June 9, 1775, in *Letters*, 6:153–54.

conscientious objection, and so forth. On the other hand, Rev 13 describes a mighty beast that raises up to challenge the authority of God, waging war and seeking to destroy God's peaceful kingdom. Historically, this beast has been interpreted as a nation-state, particularly as the Roman Empire, but also as any government or governing leader that claims to have ultimate authority and does not recognize the ultimate power of God.

Wesley the Tory certainly leaned in the direction of Rom 13, yet even he could see the beastly nature of government when he observed the slave trade or the scarcity of food. Likewise, Roberts was no anarchist. His default position was to submit to the laws of the land, but he assisted a growing protest movement when faced with injustice. Both men found themselves agreeing with Saint Peter and the other apostles when they declared, "We must obey God rather than men" (Acts 5:29).

Certainly, as Wesleyans we must value peace, but peace without justice is not true peace. Therefore, in the framework of a Wesleyan political theology, the default position is obedience and submission to the law of the land. However, if that law violates the higher law of love, then as Christians we are obligated to do what we must in order to work for justice on behalf of the oppressed. Sadly, many white Christians sat at the sidelines throughout the civil rights movement of the 1960s while the Christian minister Martin Luther King Jr. led a peaceful march toward a just peace. At the time, many "good citizens" justified their passivity by saying that they did not wish to disturb the peace, perhaps even appealing to texts such as Rom 13. Yet even the Apostle Paul himself wrote, "Let no debt remain outstanding, except the continuing debt to love one another, for whoever loves others has fulfilled the law" (Rom 13:8). This is the *highest* law; this is the guide for politics strangely warmed: it puts people before partisanship, it ranks love above law, and it demands allegiance to Christ above allegiance to country.

Bibliography

Benson, Lee. *Merchants, Farmers, and Railroads: Railroad Regulation and New York Politics, 1850–1887*. Cambridge: Harvard University Press, 1955.

Buck, Solon Justus. *The Granger Movement: A Study of Agricultural Organization and Its Political, Economic, and Social Manifestations, 1870–1880*. Lincoln: University of Nebraska, 1965.

Byrant, Barry E. "Original Sin." In *The Oxford Handbook of Methodist Studies*, edited by William J. Abraham and James E. Kirby, 522–39. Oxford: Oxford University Press, 2009.

Chinni, Dante. "Are Occupy Wall Street, Tea Party Signs of Building Populist Movements?" *PBS News Hour*, October 11, 2011. http://www.pbs.org/newshour/rundown/2011/10/are-occupy-wall-street-protests-tea-party-signs-of-populist-uprisings-to-come.html.

Dayton, Donald. *Discovering an Evangelical Heritage*. New York: Harper and Row, 1976.

Ely, James W. *Railroads and American Law*. Lawrence: University Press of Kansas, 2001.

Finke, Roger, and Rodney Stark. *The Churching of America, 1776–2005: Winners and Losers in Our Religious Economy*. 2nd ed. New Brunswick: Rutgers University Press, 2005.

Goodwyn, Lawrence. *The Populist Moment: A Short History of the Agrarian Revolt in America*. Oxford: Oxford University Press, 1978.

Halévy, Élie. *The Birth of Methodism in England*. Edited and translated by Bernard Semmel. Chicago: Chicago University Press, 1971.

Hatch, Nathan O. *The Democratization of American Christianity*. New Haven: Yale University Press, 1989.

Hicks, John D. *The Populist Revolt: A History of the Farmers' Alliance and the People's Party*. Lincoln: University of Nebraska Press, 1961.

Hogue, Wilson T. *History of the Free Methodist Church of North America*. 2 vols. Chicago: Free Methodist, 1918.

Hosman, Glenn Burton. "The Problem of Church and State in the Thought of John Wesley as Reflecting His Understanding of Providence and His View of History." PhD diss., Drew University, 1970.

Hynson, Leon O. "Human Liberty as a Divine Right: A Study in the Political Maturation of John Wesley." *Journal of Church and State* 25 (1983) 57–85.

―――. "John Wesley and Political Reality." *Methodist History* 12 (1973) 37–42.

―――. "John Wesley's Concept of Liberty of Conscience." *Wesleyan Theological Journal* 7 (1972) 36–46.

Jennings, Theodore W. *Good News to the Poor: John Wesley's Evangelical Economics.* Nashville, TN: Abingdon, 1990.

Kostlevy, William C. "Benjamin Titus Roberts and the 'Preferential Option for the Poor' in the Early Free Methodist Church." In *Poverty and Ecclesiology: Nineteenth Century Evangelicals in the Light of Liberation Theology*, edited by Anthony L. Dunnavant, 51–67. Collegeville, MN: Liturgical, 1992.

Maddox, Randy. "Nurturing the New Creation: Reflections on a Wesleyan Trajectory." In *Wesleyan Perspectives on the New Creation*, edited by M. Douglas Meeks, 21–52. Nashville, TN: Kingswood, 2004.

―――. *Responsible Grace: John Wesley's Practical Theology.* Nashville, TN: Abingdon, 1994.

―――. "Visit the Poor: Wesley's Precedent for Wholistic Mission." *Transformation: An International Dialogue on Mission and Ethics* 18 (2001) 37–50.

Madron, Thomas. "John Wesley on Economics." In *Sanctification and Liberation: Liberation Theologies in Light of the Wesleyan Tradition*, edited by Theodore Runyon, 102–15. Nashville, TN: Abingdon, 1981.

Magnusson, Norris. *Salvation in the Slums: Evangelical Social Work, 1865–1920.* Metuchen, NJ: Scarecrow, 1977.

Marquardt, Manfred. *John Wesley's Social Ethics: Praxis and Principles.* Translated by John E. Steely and W. Stephen Gunter. Nashville, TN: Abingdon, 1992.

Marston, Leslie. *From Age to Age a Living Witness: A Historical Interpretation of Free Methodism's First Century.* Winona Lake: IN: Light and Life, 1960.

McMath, Robert C. *American Populism: A Social History, 1877–1898.* New York: Hill and Wang, 1993.

Moltmann, Jürgen. *The Trinity and the Kingdom of God.* London: SCM, 1981.

Noll, Mark A. *America's God: From Jonathan Edwards to Abraham Lincoln.* New York: Oxford University Press, 2002.

Phillips, Elizabeth. *Political Theology: A Guide for the Perplexed.* New York: T. & T. Clark, 2012.

Postel, Charles. *The Populist Vision.* New York: Oxford University Press, 2007.

Rauschenbusch, Walter. *Christianity and the Social Crisis in the Twenty-first Century.* Edited by Paul Rauscenbusch. New York: HarperCollins, 2007.

Roberts, B. T. *First Lessons on Money.* Rochester, NY: B. T. Roberts, 1886.

―――. *Fishers of Men.* Winona Lake, IN: Light and Life, 1948.

―――. *Holiness Teachings: The Life and Work of B. T. Roberts.* North Chili, NY: Earnest Christian, 1893.

————. *Pungent Truths, Being Extracts from the Writings of B. T. Roberts, A.M., While Editor of "The Free Methodist" from 1886 to 1890.* Edited by W. B. Rose. Chicago: Free Methodist, 1912.

————. *Why Another Sect: Containing a Review of Articles by Bishop Simpson and Others in the Free Methodist Church.* Rochester, NY: The Earnest Christian, 1879.

————, ed. "Renting Pews." *The Earnest Christian.* June 1872. Marston Memorial Historical Society, Indianapolis, IN. http://fmcusa.org/historical/collections-3/earnest-christian/.

Root, F. P. "Origin of the Farmer's Alliance." *Cultivator and Country Gentleman* 55 (1890) 1016.

Scott, Peter, and William T. Cavanaugh. *The Blackwell Companion to Political Theology.* Blackwell Companions to Religion. Malden, MA: Blackwell, 2004.

Smith, Timothy. *Revivalism and Social Reform: American Protestantism on the Eve of the Civil War.* Gloucester, MA: Peter Smith, 1976.

Snyder, Howard A. "How B. T. Roberts Voted." In *Free Methodist Historical Society Newsletter* 9 (2008). http://fmcusa.org/historical/files/2011/06/Summer2008.pdf

————. *Populist Saints: B. T. and Ellen Roberts and the First Free Methodists.* Grand Rapids: Eerdmans, 2006.

————. *Salvation Means Creation Healed: The Ecology of Sin and Grace; Overcoming the Divorce between Earth and Heaven.* Eugene, OR: Cascade, 2011.

Vickers, Jason. *Wesley: A Guide for the Perplexed.* New York: Continuum, 2009.

————. "Wesley's Theological Emphases." In *The Cambridge Companion to John Wesley,* edited by Randy Maddox and Jason Vickers, 190–206. New York: Cambridge University Press, 2010.

Wall, Robert W. "The Embourgeoisement of the Free Methodist Ethos." *Wesleyan Theological Journal* 25 (1990) 117–29.

Ward, Graham. *The Politics of Discipleship: Becoming Postmaterial Citizens.* Grand Rapids: Baker, 2009.

Weber, Theodore R. *Politics in the Order of Salvation: Transforming Wesleyan Political Ethics.* Nashville, TN: Abingdon, 2001

Wesley, John. *The Bicentennial Edition of the Works of John Wesley.* Edited by Frank Baker and Richard P. Heitzenrater. Nashville, TN: Abingdon, 1976.

————. *The Letters of the Rev. John Wesley.* Edited by John Telford. London: Epworth, 1931.

————. *The Works of John Wesley.* Edited by Thomas Jackson. 14 vols. CD-ROM. Nashville, TN: Abingdon, 2005.

Woodward, C. Vann. *Origins of the New South, 1877–1913.* Baton Rouge: Louisiana State University Press, 1971.

Wright, N. T. *Surprised by Hope: Rethinking Heaven, the Resurrection, and the Mission of the Church.* New York: Harper Collins, 2008.

Zinn, Howard. *A People's History of the United States.* New York: HarperCollins, 2010.